Thank you for everything

T5-CCN-758

A Light in the Cave

Isobel Mitton

Isobel Mitton

A Light in the Cave

Isobel Mitton

Copyright.

"What are you going to do with all your pain?"

"I'm going to share it with the world," Isobel.

To Megan,

Thank you for everything. I am grateful for you.

From Misty

Contents

Chapter 1

The War

My grandma's energy never wavers, scatters or disappears. On perfect days, when everything is right with God and the world, it is a flawless, human shaped, bright, blue light. At times like these however, when she's visibly angry, it's almost like a detonated nuclear weapon. It keeps the force within its rigid boundaries and yet, still manages to execute with a destructive power. My grandma's a warrior without fear.

"People are cruel," she noted. "There was no need for this."

I agreed. My grandma and I are in sync. Despite being generations apart, our experiences of humanity are one and the same.

The Story Teller, a calmer energy compared to grandma, stood behind her, instructing her on how to reprogram the weapons of destruction Musa embedded in my aura when he was doing rituals on me for my final transcension in witchdoctoring. Destroying them wasn't an option. We can't make our own, nor are we allowed to, unlike Dark witchdoctors.

Mother Nature, in her wisdom allows us to use the same weapons turned against us, if we can harness and send them back where they came from. How else can we take them out of the atmosphere? Once a weapon has been constructed and sent into the wind, it can never be destroyed. It remains in the stratosphere, growing in strength and striking at innocent bystanders.

If we can send it back to its maker, we take it out of circulation.

The weapons were sent to me by Musa. They did their job. They plunged me into emotional and psychological chaos. It didn't take too long for the metaphysical to go three dimensional on me. The physical effects were mostly sexual in nature. His weapons kept me scratching at my inner thighs all night long. They were crawling their way to my vagina. Sexual organs are an important area to witchdoctors of the dark. Where there's sex, there's money and power. They want both. Taking it from you is as simple as controlling your sexuality.

Sexual attacks, whether it be taking your vagina out of action or sending bad spirits to fuck you while you sleep are such a dark witchdoctor thing to do.

Musa was brilliant. His weapons were good. First, he got me all confused, physically dizzy, depressed and desperate before he launched the sex thing. He followed it up with the greatest theft.

6

Too bad for him we found him out before he rejoiced in his success. Well, he was gonna have what he worked hard on, times one hundred. Witchdoctors of Light have the power to strengthen dark witchdoctors' weapons to a nuclear level.

It sounds easy, right? Except Dark witchdoctors have amazing defence grids against backlash. Their defence mechanisms are far superior in comparison to ours. To make matters more difficult, Musa was a defence and protection expert. There was a thousand percent chance Musa would remain untouched.

His capability was the reason I went to him in the first place, besides him being in charge of my final transcension ritual. His job was to create an impenetrable defence shield for me. He executed excellently while leaving a back door for him to get at me. I didn't know this little fact at the time. Through the back door, he sent spells to grind me to dust.

Basically, I had no protection. I was as vulnerable as I'd always been. Easy pickings. He selected what he wanted, intending to take everything. The banquet was too scintillating to leave even a morsel.

Our plan of attack was as old as time. We were going to blast Musa's protection with our own chants before we sent his weapons back to him. It was tough work. Grandma said we were built for this. I wasn't sure. In my head, I was constructed for something else and it had nothing to do with the metaphysical.

The metaphysical always surprised me. The rules were not carefully written on stone. Everything depended on an individual's right to choose. Yet, I hadn't chosen this. Who wants to die over and over? Transcension is death. You go through rituals which bring you into the veil. When you come out of the veil the next day, you're a completely different person. What was true of you the day before isn't today.

During my first visit into the veil, I learned everyone whom I adored, didn't feel the same way about me. Vision after vision of my loved ones doing and saying things against me brutally assailed me, giving me no respite. I saw and heard conversations about me which I wasn't privy to in the physical. I tasted and smelled the hate, contempt, envy, jealousy and greed towards me. I was devastated. I crawled out of the metaphysical clutching painful truth. The road to acceptance was hard and bumpy.

When I floated back into the veil the second time, it deigned to reveal I was three decades off my life plan as per God. The life that was meant to be mine, versus the one man made for me played out in technicolor detail. Goals I was supposed to meet, places I should've gone, love, marriage and children I was meant to have, all there, on display in the form of a movie. The veil don't play. It juxtaposed what should've been with what was, tearing my soul to pieces. The final truth was basic, everything that was meant to be mine was now beyond me. Never to be retrieved.

The hate, contempt, envy, jealousy and greed had destroyed my life. Everything was stripped from me by those who pretended to love me. They left me an empty shell, barren to the end. I grieved. There was no comfort to be had.

My dreams were simple. I was going to be an average journalist, marry an accountant, have three children and lived the average middleclass lifestyle among my people. I was going to fill my three-bedroom home with love. How could this vision of my life have threatened anyone? Why did they take it from me?

I writhed on my belly, using my fingers to drag my body forward and out of the veil. I couldn't stand. Working towards healing, after this knowledge was cemented into my reality, is a work in progress.

On this last transcension, I glided into the veil afraid of what was in store for me. What came through was the one thing I never thought would happen. I lost my identity. Poof! It was gone in a puff of smoke, leaving me radarless.

I was born to the Shona, a grouping of fourteen smaller tribes. They came together, hundreds of years before colonization and decided to create a "United States." Different tribes sharing one language and one God. My particular subgroup, the Zezuru have a formidable and envious history. They were warriors, both men and women. They believed in equality of the sexes and lived their truth. They came from East Africa, incorporated other tribes as they made their way down and proceeded to amass a lot of territory in what is now present-day Zimbabwe through warfare.

More importantly, they were led by my direct lineage. My family was their royal family. There are cities named after them, including the capital city of Zimbabwe, Harare. I was born a princess with the cultural trappings of such.

The veil disagreed with my identity. I was Xhosa, it said. From the Eastern Cape. My last name wasn't mine and my first name was wrong. It belonged to the tribe of my birth and not my bloodline.

A single day of paying homage to my Xhosa ancestors via the Shona way would be sacrilegious. I was to adjust forthwith. I stumbled out of the veil, shocked. And then I laughed for days. How else could I process this?

In one day, everything was stripped from me. It's like learning you're European when you know you're African. You look African, sound African, think African. You've got to be who you know you are! Umm, no. You're European. It doesn't matter who you think you are when your blood says otherwise. Your ancestors are Xhosa little girl. Deal.

I was born again. There are no words to describe this catastrophe.

If Metaphysical rules were written on stone like the ten commandments, Musa might not have got away with declaring himself a witchdoctor of the light. He was a high-ranking member of our organization. He represented Zimbabwe internationally on many occasions.

Only witchdoctors of light can belong to the Zimbabwe National Traditional Healers Association (ZINATHA). We are vetted, certified and educated in the Light arts. We carry the same ranking as medical doctors. We even work in tangent with medical doctors. We also deliberate in the justice system and we oversee all spiritual rituals, from rainmaking to fertility.

Musa was also recommended by the current president of ZINATHA, George, to my ancestors and I. George went to great lengths extolling Musa's abilities.

More importantly, I trusted Musa as a colleague and as an elder. I leaned on him, hoping I could learn some things. We talked over the phone for days after I got back from Zimbabwe. I hoped we could work together in order to help raise the witchdoctors of light from the depths of despair they now find themselves in our culture, due to the popularity of the dark side.

Over the years, witchdoctors of the dark have become more in number than those who fight for the light. They hold positions of power in our national organizations and the agenda leans towards their goals. Their desire is to bleed people dry and they've become experts at it.

Said people have developed bitter darkness. Everyone wants to be like Robert Mugabe. They know he used witchdoctors of the dark for his purposes, including his longevity. Chemotherapy wasn't what kept him alive all those years. The people, therefore decided to emulate their leader's "by any means necessary" motto.

If he could get away with evil spectacularly and without repercussions, they could also use evil to disappear from poverty. Fuck the consequences in the afterlife. You gotta eat another to avoid being eaten yourself. People have also learned evil pays quicker than piety. Dark skilled practitioners are in fashion.

It was no wonder I was willing to work with Musa to help raise the lot of the Light side. He said all the right things to make me believe he wanted to change the tides. My greed was another reason I went against my instincts. I desired his knowledge of the metaphysical. He seemed more than amiable to the idea of sharing.

Well, class was out. This was my graduation ceremony. This war right here, was gonna put the entire metaphysical world on notice. They were gonna know I was no longer a walkover. The little fish swimming her way up the Niagara Falls was almost there, at the apex. Gone were the days when they could do what they wanted with me. I was mistress of my domain.

No one was going to walk in and snatch any of my ancestors ever again. There were going to be no more cages for me either. Been there, done it too many times. I was never going to serve anyone on this earth or through the veil, knowingly, or unknowingly. Those days were gone. Forever.

I was gonna fight to my last breath. It was a good thing I was standing my ground with Musa, for he was at the top of the pile. Strategically, it's best to cut off the head of a snake, rather than its tail.

Honestly, I was tired of being afraid and helpless. I wasn't afraid of death. In fact, I welcomed it. It would release me from this human experience in which I was born a sacrifice. Life is what I feared. Life in bondage, pain, poverty and depravity, not of my own making.

"You're going to come out of this stronger, more knowledgeable," my grandma's voice slid into my thoughts. What goes on between grandma and I is pure telepathy. I hear her in my head, as if she's sitting next to me. Her voice is clear, distinct and very passionate. "Wars like this bring out gifts you never knew you had. Our Father endowed you with everything you need. You're His gatekeeper. His light in the cave. He knew before He put you on this earth you would be outnumbered, one hundred to one."

Light in the cave. The first witchdoctor who told me I was the Chosen said the same thing. I no longer remembered his name, but his speech stuck with me. "God fights from within. He puts a light in the darkest cave. A little flicker banishes the darkness. The stronger the light, the less darkness there is."

"I think the light needs help," was my reply.

"No," he shook his head. "We work alone because Light is the most powerful thing. Those of the dark work in groups, covens. They're weak. They instil fear in order to conquer. We encourage hope. Hope never dries up."

Yeah. I still had issues. Had God ever heard about team-work? Why did He expect a witchdoctor of the light to fight hundreds of other gifted people alone?

"A single match lit in a cave banishes the darkness forever," grandma agreed with the witchdoctor from my memory. "There's no need for overkill."

Yeah. Right. When my time came, I was gonna have words with God. None of them were going to be good.

"Don't forget your armour."

"Blue or black and white?" I asked.

"Blue. Women are the ones who defend the home. This is the girls' war. Just as well. Men are lazy. They don't see things through."

Grandma had a very low opinion of men.

"We're going to beat this Musa because he's a man. You'll see. Wrap your blue. Time to get to work. We have three hours."

I'd forgotten about time. At three in the morning, I could be forgiven. All spiritual warfare takes place between eleven thirty pm to two am for the dark side. They have a grace period afterward of fifty-nine minutes. Our time began at three am and ended at six.

Oh, the unfairness of it all! They had more hours than us! Another thing I was going to bring to God's attention.

"It's because we're stronger!" grandma insisted. "You have no idea how strong you are. Even among the fighters of light. You're the apex. You can harness, fire, wind, earth and water. All four elements. You're the queen."

I'd been told this before, not only by her. I, however, had only mastered wind, due to being caged by my enemies most of my life. I was only beginning to breathe free. Musa's attack interrupted my lessons on empowering and instructing water.

"Time, time," grandma chided.

I retrieved my blue wrap from the chair of the war room I created in my basement when this Musa thing reared its ugly head. My altar, facing the East was the center of the little corner. Since my first Transcension, I'd never had a special place to do spiritual things. I did my rituals anywhere I chose in my tiny house. In fact, I'd never used my ceremonial mat. Ever. This would be the first time.

The war with Musa brought my graduation. A war room and a permanent altar were needed. It was there I could gather all the energies available to me and we could pow wow. I was also aware dark energies would be surrounding me for some time. I wanted them in a localized place. Controlling as much as possible was necessary for everything to work in my favor.

With that in mind, I went down to my basement. My basement is unfinished, cold, dank and never used except for storage and laundry. With my compass I found the East and created my war room facing the sacred direction. In the coming weeks, my war room was going to look fierce. In that moment however, all I had was the mat rolled out, my ancestors' walking sticks, wooden plates, knobkerries and spears. On the mat were two candles, black and white, representing my male and female ancestors, and a small wooden plate filled with tobacco.

I robbed my dresser of its chair and used it to pile my armour which of course, are my ancestral colors. My materials were organized in order of importance. The black and white cloths were on top, followed by the blue of my female ancestors. The materials I used to cover my head were at the bottom.

I dragged a blue wrap, quickly tied it to my waist and covered my head. For the second time in my life, I knelt on my mat, made of reeds. The one and only time I'd done so previously was during my first transcension.

Those days when I could ignore my ancestral mat were gone now. This was a new age. I needed my throne. I lit my candles, grabbed my grandma's walking stick in both hands, made sure her knobkerrie was facing outward and I was good to go.

"Time to chant," grandma encouraged me. "Be passionate, resolute, truthful. A chant is only as good as the one giving it. It is your only weapon. It breaks open the veil and moves the elements. Be heard. Be felt. Be seen."

"Who am I talking to?"

"Mother Nature. God doesn't take sides. He loves everyone equally. Why?"

"For light to exist, there must be darkness," I muttered.

That was some bullshit! God really had to do something with himself. I wished he could live here as a human being for one day. He would change those rules after his human experience.

"Human beings eat each other. It is nature."

You don't say? It was unfortunate I was the feast for hundreds.

"You had it harder than many. You're still standing. I died. Begin your chant to Mother Nature. She takes sides. She's the judge, the jury and the executioner. She can aid or repel you. You need her on your side. Musa already stated his case. More than once. It's time to tell her your story."

I got heated. How could someone, whom I've never done shit to, get permission to enslave me?

"He put a strong case forward."

OMG, sometimes these ancestors could drive a girl insane with their one sentences.

"It doesn't matter what he said to gain permission. This is y-our moment."

"How come she never punished my parents, brother, sisters, aunts and uncles? Taurai?"

"Because you never put your case forward. You didn't know how. Now you do. Tell her."

What I would really have liked to tell Mother Nature was that taking Musa's case had made her a piece of shit in my mind. She allowed the innocent to be gouged by the guilty.

"She works with what is put in front of her," grandma insisted. My grandma hears every thought and every feeling I put out, "State your case. You're in the courts of the people."

I took a deep breath, closed my eyes and stated my case.

"Open the court first."

I'd forgotten. With this kind of thing happening, I had no hope of beating this dude. This was a very steep learning curve. "I hail the owners of this land where I live, hunt and rest. My name's Isobel, she who shepherds God's children for my people. I thank you for the kindness you bestow upon me every day on your land," I paused for respect.

"I come to you this morning with a request. In your kindness and generosity, please allow me to talk to my ancestors, they who live with me. Please permit their voices to carry in your winds, sky, earth and water in order to reach my ears. I also ask for your consent for my voice to be heard by them using the same elements."

I stopped again to ask grandma if I was doing it right.

"Yes. Tell them the purpose of the court."

"My ancestors and I would like to wage a defence war against mine own who have wronged me."

"Tell them we will not harm their earth, sky, winds and water in the process. Rather, we will cleanse it of anything our own have sent to their territory."

I repeated her words.

"Ask them for their cooperation. From now on, can they please block as much as they can of what's being sent to us from where we came from."

I said the same words.

"Ululate three times. Bow three times."

Done.

"Now tell us why you've opened the court. Invite us to the court."

Protocol is really messed up sometimes. All four of my ancestors knew why I'd opened the court. They told me to. Yet, I still had to go through the formalities.

"It has to be done to stop other uninvited spirits from joining in." Grandma gave me an explanation for the first time on why I had to give these elaborate invitations for something we decided as a group. "There are many undesignated spirits floating about, looking for things to do. They can be a help or a hindrance, depending on whether they're light or dark. This court is for family only."

I was used to inviting my ancestors, I did it without thought.

"Now, hail Mother Nature. Be a strong attorney."

Grandma couldn't give me words for Mother Nature. I had to do it myself.

"I've never knelt before you," I began. "Because I didn't know how, or even that I had to. My eyes were closed. Not by me, but by others."

I wanted to cry all of a sudden. Where had it come from, this feeling. The helplessness! I was angry at myself for not knowing I should've been talking to Mother Nature all these years. The years of agony I'd gone through could've been avoided. How could I not have known? Simple. I was born in the culture that knew this was necessary, yet no one taught me this. The evil of humanity brought those angry tears. There was no stopping them now.

"Go with it," grandma encouraged. "Let go."

"I take one step forward in this life, people bring me one hundred steps back. Or a thousand. Nothing I build ever stands. I work hard. Yet, I get nothing in return. Because I've been cursed. The curses and blockages were planted since before the day I was born. I fight against the tide and I drown. I have no one to help me. Not one aunt, uncle, sibling, cousin, parent. I'm an orphan, yet I was born to hundreds."

Yeah, I hated standing on reality.

"I've never done a single evil thing to anyone. People take from me. They've stolen my health, children I wanted to have, relationships I was in or was going to be in, my metaphysical wealth given to my soul by God, my name, my ancestors, my soul. Just when I think I've finally made it to the end of the tunnel, Musa comes along and helps himself to my ancestor. You know Mother Nature, someone like me can't survive this human experience without every single one of the ancestors given to me by God. My health will deteriorate, leading me to death or worse, a life of disability. He, like the others, knew this. Yet, he still did it."

More tears. It was hard to believe the whole world wanted you dead. It was even harder to come to terms with it when those who wanted you dead the most, were the ones you loved, respected or looked up to.

"Keep going," grandma pushed.

"Musa stole my ancestor. For his clairvoyance and the other gifts he bestows on me. In the process, he gagged my grandma and sought to enslave my soul. He did it because he thought I was stupid. He decided God above had not known what he was doing when he picked my soul as the Chosen."

"Good," my grandma whispered in my head. "Remember the Fire!"

Oh yes, fire. The thing was, the tears were still in charge.

"Water will be fine too," grandma gave up on me finding the flame.

Just as well.

"This isn't the first time this has happened to me. Every time someone does this to me, it destroys me. Makes me want to turn dark. I want to kill the whole world!"

Bitch better look at my life. I knew what she would see. Nothing but broken pieces of hope.

"I have nothing. They left me bare, inhuman."

The tears. They came in buckets. I wailed inconsolably for several minutes. This world was cold man. And the human experience was the worst ever.

"At some point, we all have to make a stand. This is mine!" I screamed this out loud.

"Excellent!"

"I'm done with being the walking dead."

"Very good!" continued grandma's commentary.

"I therefore accuse Musa of theft, avarice and all the other deadly sins I can't remember. For that, I declare war on him and everyone who has lifted their weapon against me. Be it in the past, present or future."

I was going to fight them all. Might as well. I suddenly felt tired of this conversation. Had I done enough? Perhaps not. One more thing, straight from my heart. "Mother Nature, I understand why I'm the sacrifice from my clan, yet, I have gone through a lot. Even for a Chosen. Show mercy on my soul by giving me justice. There has to be justice."

Not enough. She needed more. I sensed it. I breathed out unsteadily, all the injustice in my life rushed in and took residence. "My mother was the first to steal the Story Teller when I was 12 and

I ended up in bed, unable to walk for a year. Then my father stole him when I was in my early twenties. As a result, all my relationships with men and my career were ruined. My cousin Taurai came after him too when I was in my forties. His actions cost me years of my life where I lay in bed, unable to move and soiling myself in the worst of times."

It came to me that stating my case in its entirety was a good move. I was going to get what I wanted from Mother Nature, no matter what.

"And then there were fellow witchdoctors. Molly, my ascension witchdoctor, not only tried to steal him, she also sent evil spirits my way. She tried to kill me. The first zombies I ever saw were from her."

I genuinely liked Molly. I'd never met a female witchdoctor like her. She dazzled me. Molly had a powerful presence aided by her six feet tall frame in a country of five feet three- inch males. She could've done with dropping a few pounds like the rest of us, except, her height helped carry her extremely wide girth better than mine ever could. Compounded with the energy she exuded; she was more than a goddess to me. She had the "sistas can do it for themselves thing." It was truly an aphrodisiac for someone like me. She made me believe all things were possible and I'd finally reached utopia.

She was also beautiful and naughty as hell. Prone to pick pocketing, she met her husband while in a jail cell and spent most of her twenties and thirties as a cop's wife. I met her after his death.

Molly was constantly surrounded by women. This wasn't surprising, considering her energy. She walked the earth with a male ancestor whom I saw with my own eyes. I could see where Molly got her mischief from.

I overlooked the little things about her personality which gave me pause. For instance, she spoke to the women who followed her as if they were her servants. She referred to us as her sheep, a derogatory and submissive term with so many hidden connotations of metaphysical slavery.

In my idolization mode, I saw it as a compliment. I desperately wanted to belong. More importantly, I needed a mentor. Molly was just the right person to take me under her wing because she continued to work with the female witchdoctors she helped transcend long after their ascension. Her speciality were women like me, those of us who came to our purpose later in life because of one reason or another. She taught us the basics of reaching out to our ancestors. She was the first one to tell me ancestors could only be reached at three in the morning. I also had to face the East when I talked to them. All this time, I'd been doing it wrong. I spent years "talking" to my ancestors with my back turned to the East and at convenient times of my own. My ancestors and I didn't connect until Molly taught me the right way.

When we were attacked by dark forces, Molly was there, doing spells on our behalf to keep us safe. All she required in return was complete loyalty. It was easy to give.

When another woman warned me about her, I didn't listen. She said Molly wasn't who I believed her to be.

"Be careful," the woman urged.

I was loyal, I reported the conversation to Molly verbatim. She was furious.

Another said to me, "awful things happen to people when Molly gets angry at them. She destroys lives."

What she said went in one ear and came out the other. If I saw signs of her true personality, I ignored them. I wanted to live in Molly's world. She was the sun. I needed to feel warm. Then she stole my ancestor and crippled me. The irony of it all. She saved me from one witchdoctor, only to do what he did to me.

"Now this. I discovered the Story Teller was missing via a reading by another witchdoctor. It's been a month since my last and final ritual of ascension. You see, I learned from the last time with Molly. I resolved to always get another witchdoctor to check out my metaphysical after a month of rituals."

It wasn't what the witchdoctor said. It was what he didn't say. He didn't see the Story Teller. And he told me grandma was gagged. He didn't see the gagging as a problem for we came from two different Bantu cultures. I did.

I went through the notes from the reading at night, looking for discrepancies, and bingo, there were many. In the first place, why was grandma restricted? She was the voice of my ancestors. She needed to talk!

Her being muzzled meant someone wanted to keep their secret. What secret? The question kept me awake, hammering away in my brain constantly. It didn't take too long for it to hit me. Grandma being gagged was the least of my worries. I was missing one whole ancestor. The Story Teller.

In panic, I called my bestie, regardless of the late night. Agnes picked up at once. I explained the situation. "Grandma has been gagged because someone stole the Story Teller! Who would do this?"

I started screaming, out of my mind. This couldn't be happening again. Oh no, no, NO!

"Calm down," Agnes advised.

How could I calm down? This was a catastrophe of great proportions.

"Oh my God, how could people do this to me?" I wailed, bereft. "How did this happen? I'm supposed to be stronger."

I worked my way into a frenzy. What was I going to do?

"They're gonna keep doing this to me," I sobbed hysterically. My tears were definitely angry ones. "How can people be so cruel? So vicious?"

"There's a positive here. You discovered it early. This means you're stronger. It took you forever with Taurai and it was obvious to everyone he envied and hated you. Then with Molly, it was months before you realized what she was up to. With your new metaphysical strength, you can beat this."

Agnes is a social worker. It's her job to use common sense. She is Oprah to my Gayle. We've been inseparable since we met ten years ago.

"I'm tired," I cried. The exhaustion was deep. "I'm tired. My soul can't take anymore."

"You're a fighter by nature. I've seen you fight institutions and win. You represent the little people. You'll catch the thief and get the Story Teller back. You've always done it. Get some sleep. Rest. You'll figure things out tomorrow."

"In the physical world I fix shit, because I have experience. In the metaphysical, I'm the new kid on the block," I added truth to the matter.

"No one learns better or faster than you. You're smarter than all those people who reside in the metaphysical. You are that bitch and always have been. You can do this. Get some rest. Tomorrow is another day."

"Nope. I give up. I'm not going to fight for the Story Teller. Completely. They can have him. I can't do this anymore. I take one step forward and they take me ten steps back."

"You don't mean it. You have the soul of a warrior. Like your grandma," Agnes was positive.

"No!" It hurt to fight. "They win. I concede."

I took defeat to bed. Sleep was as elusive as the Peak where God resided. I tortured myself, something I'm very good at.

"How could this happen? How did it happen? Why? When? Where? Who?" Oh fuck. Same old shit, different time, different players. Why was I thinking about it? I'd given up on the metaphysical after all. It was about time.

Three am came and went with me resisting the altar. Those ancestors who allowed themselves to be stolen could fuck off for all I cared. Didn't they understand how hard my life was?

They understood, a breeze curled around me, bringing a reply from the veil. Along with the response were images I knew well. A story unfolded. My grandma was beaten to death by her own brother, after he stole her harvest. Her only crime, according to my village was having the nerve to ask for her harvest back. She was a woman, they said. She should've known her place. She got what she deserved.

When my grandma divorced my grandfather, she became a pariah. Furthermore, her independent and hardworking spirit made the men in her family jealous and envious. The envy turned to hate. Hate became murder and no one gave a damn because she was a woman. Had it been the other way around, she would've been executed.

The Story Teller was poisoned due to his position in the royal court. He died a gruesome and painful death at the age of thirty-six. Afterwards, his wife, girlfriends, children, friends and whomever he left behind were slaughtered. A quiet servant girl however, kept her mouth shut about the baby in her belly. His line continued. His lineage produced me because his son lay quietly in his momma's womb during the carnage.

My grief was deep as the story played out to its conclusion. This shit happened to real people. My family. And here I was, abandoning them at the first sign of trouble. No. By five am, I'd decided to retrieve my family from whomever. The veil had refused to let me give up.

My grandma was my best friend. Bar none. The quiet, stoic Story Teller who sees through people and dissects situations in seconds was my calming place, my protection and my trail blazer. These energies were a part of me. I was born to them and they were given to me by God before I became human, making them my longest relationships. I loved them.

A familiar indignant anger rose. No one was going to get away with stealing The Story Teller or gagging my grandma. I was going to fight them. I didn't take my declaration lightly.

The Metaphysical is a dangerous world. Full of more darkness than light. Many witchdoctors of light have lost their lives fighting the dark side. Victory was never guaranteed. And here I was, a witchdoctor of a mere few years, compared to those who'd been in the game since they were children. I was taking on the titans. My failure rate, on paper, was high.

Just as fear overwhelmed me, threatening to break my resolve, I remembered the true physical scientific point of light eradicating darkness. When a little light flickered, no matter how dark the space, it tore through everything, illuminating the heavens themselves. Besides, I was the strongest witchdoctor there was, as decided by God Himself. I'd witnessed my own feats and marveled at what I could do.

I was no longer afraid.

Who the fuck had done it anyway? The first question I needed answered was also the most important. Waging war against an unknown was prohibited. Mother Nature needed to know who the culprit was for her to allow you to send volleys in her space.

I needed the culprit. Unfortunately, grandma couldn't tell me. The gag must've taken effect a day or two before I saw the witch-doctor who revealed it, because all this time, she'd been talking. We'd been working together. Now, however, there was complete silence. I was on my own. A place I knew very well.

I ran down the usual suspects. My mother. My dad was dead. My cousin Taurai. He still wanted the Story Teller. All five of the witchdoctors who'd helped in my ascension. There was the old lady, who'd seen much of my life and helped me get rid of excess, opportunistic spirits. Gushungo, who turned out to be my favorite because we shared similar philosophies on belonging to the community.

Was it Shoko? He asked me out as soon as his ritual with me was done. Or was it Musa who gave me the whole professionalism speech? There was also Jimmy, the one who embraced the Apostolic Faith belief systems and helped hundreds in his community. It could've been any one of them.

It could've been my aunt Retina whom I stayed with at the village. My father's younger brother and all my cousins were suspects. The choice of me as a conduit enraged them. For years, while my dad was alive, they helped him sabotage me. I was sure they continued after he passed.

My mother's family in general were all suspects too. Good God up above, it could be anyone. How was I going to find out?

It came to me, out of the blue. The gym. Physical activity o-pened the veil. I was gonna have to step into it in order to ungag my grandma. Damn! I hadn't been going to the gym on the regular. I was weak. I wasn't even sure I could last on the treadmill for ten minutes. A good hour was required at a jogging pace of four point two, in order to break through the veil.

I was gonna do it. The end.

I hit the treadmill, to the protest of my thighs. I ran as fast as I could while I talked to grandma. I told her how much I loved her. Without hearing her voice every morning, life would be unbearab-le.

I was literally huffing and puffing like the three-little piggy's in the Fairy tale. Light appeared. It was a mere sliver, yet I was thrilled. I'd broken the veil. Now I had to open it wide. I jogged faster, ho-ping my heart wouldn't give out on me.

"Grandma!" I called out in my mind, but I muttered it aloud. "You're the oldest. The strongest. The most righteous. Whoever has done this to you, has nothing on you. You're pure light. You cannot be gagged or destroyed."

The veil broke wide! Light rushed towards me. Followed by an eerie silence as it bathed me, drew me in.

"Remove the gag. No one can put you in chains."

Still more silence. Grandma needed help. The spell was too strong.

"I call upon the winds, water, sky, soil! I call upon the good spirits of the continuum! Help us. Ungag my grandmother."

Something. A shade of blue crept into the light.

"Let there be fire. Destroy the bad magic, burn it to ash so grandma can be free! I call upon the good who're still walking. Help us."

"This time, it's different," her wonderful voice invaded my head a minute or two later.

Jogging continued. I was afraid to stop as hard as it was to keep going. What if the portal closed?

"It's different," she said again. There, she'd made it. The gag was gone.

I broke into a flood of tears. Right there. In front of fitness fanatics.

"What do you mean?" I stopped jogging. There was no need anymore.

"It's not family."

"Who is it then?"

"A witchdoctor."

I named them, one by one until I got to Musa.

"Yes, him."

I was stunned. Although I shouldn't have been. Of all the witchdoctors I met, he was my least favorite. I almost refused to work with him. Nevertheless, my ancestors chose him for a reason. I went through with it. In trust.

"Why?"

"For many reasons. He wanted the Story Teller for his gifts and you."

"Me?"

"He wanted to own you. Make you work for him."

Slavery exists in the metaphysical world. A witchdoctor can harness the gifts of another and use them to their benefit. They do this by caging your soul in the veil.

This is how it translates on the ground. Everything the caged person touches turns to dust. For every hour of work put into their passion, money is given to the witchdoctor holding the key. The hours of their labor are calculated in the metaphysical, turned to coin and the keyholder gets some kind of windfall. This has happened to me before. Many times. I'm an experienced ex slave. I've been caged all my life.

My mother was my first master, followed by my dad, then Nyanzira, a member of my mom's coven and a witchdoctor, who then pulled in Taurai, my cousin. For seven years, Taurai held the keys to my life before I broke free with the help of Molly. Molly, who then turn around and tried to thrust me into cage of her own making. It never ends.

Musa wanting to enslave me didn't make sense. As part of the spell of enslavement, the slave must need the slave master in some way. There must be a relationship on the physical plane where the slave needs the master.

My parents fed, educated and housed me. It was easy for them. Nyanzira came to me as a savior. Taurai lavished me with gifts and Molly simply tried to force me to admit I was her sheep.

Of all the witchdoctors I used, I hadn't needed Musa at all. In fact, on the occasions we talked, I was doing him favors. I should've enslaved him. How could it be him then? He hadn't enacted the process in the physical of ownership of another soul.

"The dreams," grandma said. "You called him twice after you had those dreams, asking for help."

Those damn dreams! They had me all hysterical in the middle of the night. They were so vivid, like a horror movie. The first one was about my son's soul being stolen. It reduced me to ashes.

I felt powerless, bereft. Gushungo came to mind immediately. He would know what to do. He could instruct me on how to save my son.

Gushungo didn't pick up my frantic calls. I tried a dozen times until I flopped back on my bed, helpless. Out of nowhere, a gentle voice in the stillness of my room whispered, "Musa."

No. Everything within me clenched in rejection. Then I felt guilty. What had made me react this way to a man who'd done nothing to me? I talked myself into calling.

He put me to shame. He was very caring and full of assurances. Of course, he was gonna help me protect my son. I did a very good thing in coming to him because he saw me like a little sister. I was very important to him, dear to his heart.

What he said didn't ring true. Again, my soul rejected him. Nevertheless, if he chose to see me as his sister, it was all good. He could help with the protection of my son without malice.

He said he would send me some extremely powerful herbs for an exorbitant fee.

"I'm sorry to charge you such an amount my sister, after all the help you've given me. My time must be paid for, however," His tone was oily, almost mean.

Wow, I found myself thinking, this is what you do for a sister? Charge her thousands after all the free help she gave you with your metaphysical issues? Hmm.

Grandma said no deal. "He is a last resort."

I was down with that.

As I lay in my bed after my conversation with Musa, a voice from the past came through.

"You have the power to heal your son yourself," Nyanzira said.

Nyanzira was a witchdoctor who gone bad with time. He started out a warrior of light, decided it didn't pay enough and ditched it for darkness. He was therefore twice as lethal as the average dark practitioner. He damaged me a lot in the metaphysical. It translated to the physical in double time with terrible consequences. He first worked with my mother and siblings. He was their go-to guy. Their witchdoctor in the "Let's kill Isobel parade." At some point, he changed allegiances to work with my cousin Taurai, who wanted my ancestors as well as my metaphysical wealth. His motive for switching was simple. Taurai had more money than my mother.

Taurai took to visiting me every two months or so. His trips were always the same. He first went to Zimbabwe, then crossed to Canada before going to his England.

We became very close. We talked on skype for hours on end daily. I shared my confusing metaphysical world with him without leaving out a single thing. As my ancestors were still suppressed and blocked by my mother, what I received from the veil was jumbled. Occasionally, they would temporarily break through. Taurai was the one I called to help me make sense of everything. He was my blood. I trusted him.

Dumb, right? We sent each other birthday gifts and took holidays together. I adored my cousin. He was a bright light in my dark world.

His visits were a highlight of mine. Only later did I learn he needed to take my personal items, have me touch his forehead and chant in my house while I was asleep. All his visits were to do with transferring my ancestors and metaphysical wealth from me to him. He paid Nyanzira half a million British pounds for his expertise.

Taurai was a very educated high earner from a once wealthy and politically powerful family. He had it together, more than me, or so I believed. After all, I was the poor cousin, a single mother and a family outcast, whereas he was in upper crust society, mingling with titled people in England. I felt honored he was my family. I sucked up to him a lot.

Not to mention he was the boy I used to wake up at three am to play with as part of my servitude to his family. I mothered him, even though I was only seven years older. The bonds, on my side were strong.

It never crossed my mind he would stoop to such a terrible level, at my expense. Fortunately for me, as time went on, he made mistakes. His jealousy and envy of me made it impossible for him to execute Nyanzira's instructions efficiently.

Nyanzira eventually decided he'd been paid enough by Taurai and didn't need him anymore to finish off his plans. He dropped him and put in his bid to be my master. Boy was he good! He was the best of them all. Of course, he had plenty of time to study and experiment on my schematics.

When he was ready to strike, he approached me himself, no longer hiding in Taurai's shadow. What a great time too! I'd been laid up, ill from an unknown cause for weeks straight. He told me I was sick because my mother was out to get my ass. He'd been working with her. Eventually, he felt sorry for me. He'd come to help me. All I had to do was accept my purpose.

"Do you know why you should accept your purpose?" The suave man in his late thirties asked me over a phone call.

"Why?"

"All witchdoctors are born to dark practitioners. God fights from within. In a dark cave, he lights a match. You're the torchbearer, sent to get rid of your mother's darkness. As I was. As we all were. At the moment, your mother is holding onto your ancestors. She's using them. If you don't accept your purpose, she will kill you."

"What difference would it make if I accept my purpose?" I wasn't interested in the metaphysical. At all.

"No one will be able to do spells on you. You will be strong and safe."

Great deal.

"What do I have to do?"

"That's where I come in. I'll help you with your first transcension. It will enable your ancestors to move from your mother to you."

"I can't come to Zimbabwe for the seven-day ritual. I'm broke and I'm sick."

"Don't worry about the illness. I'm going to help you reverse those spells. And you don't have to come. I can do it by myself. As long as you send the money for what is needed, I am driven to help you. You're an amazing light. The brightest we have. You're in fact, the apex."

Someone actually wanted to help me! Elation. I agreed. Not knowing the whole story. Nyanzira couldn't take my ancestors from my mother, but he could take them from me. Since ancestors are for sale in Africa, I imagine he wanted to sell them. After all, my cousin Taurai bought my ancestors for half a million British pounds.

"We should do this quickly. Your mother's desperate to see you dead," Nyanzira urged.

That wasn't a lie. She told me herself. She came to visit me in Canada when I wasn't feeling well. Her excitement at my illness, noted by my two besties, was very macabre. Her eyes shone with happiness when she saw I couldn't move from the couch because my body ached.

"We can hardly wait for you to die!" she gushed. "We will have a huge funeral for you."

"I want to be cremated," I said. "And I don't want anyone to know I am gone until way after. Perhaps three months later. I want to go quietly."

"No!" the woman we called Chairman Mao, after the communist Chinese leader shrieked. "You will be buried the way I want. Everyone will be invited."

How could I deny Nyanzira's truth?

"Trust me," he was very charming. "I will free you from your mother's evil."

Thinking about Nyanzira literally hurts my heart. The heart breaks physically from emotional anguish. It will kill you. Facts.

"Get back to the dreams," grandma urged. She was well aware of how my heart transferred everything from the metaphysical to the physical. It worried her. Plus, there wasn't time for that now as I was laying out the facts of my life to Mother Nature.

The second dream was about my relatives in the village. The dream unveiled a couple of male cousins taking money from me by force. I fought back, snatching my purse from them in rage.

"This is my purse! You can't have it."

I proceeded to give one of them a good thrashing. A boy of about twelve entered the scene. Behind him was a face closely resembling Musa. The face spoke.

"These are the people you love he asked, the ones who steal your metaphysical wealth while you suffer?"

I woke up. I constantly dream about people stealing from me. In reality, people steal from me too. Money, equipment, any businesses I dare to start, my books, you name it. It's an ongoing problem without end. The dream, therefore, didn't make an impact.

What interested me more was the face and the boy. They were familiar to me. Where had I met them? And what the heck were they doing in a dream about my cousins? It took me a few days to realize the boy was Musa's son. I met him on the day of my ritual. The man's face therefore had to be Musa.

My grandma insisted we do a ritual at three am asking Musa to politely leave our dreams and never come back.

He didn't listen. He was on a roll. I was so over him when he invaded my dreams for the third time. In fact, I told him so, in the dream. On this occasion, he played a young, handsome witchdoctor. He was dressed in all our traditional regalia, the feathered headdress and breechcloth, leaving magnificent abs on show. The man exuded sex appeal from hundreds of years ago. He was going for sexual attraction, hoping I lose my wits from lust.

The witchdoctor sat across from his plate of tobacco, ready to open the courts of the Bantus for me. A young boy, of about twelve acted as his assistant.

I didn't buy it for a second. Musa went to a lot of trouble creating this little scenario. Unfortunately, he forgot to camouflage his son's face. The Devil's in the details people! I rushed into the set up and kicked the plate of tobacco to high heaven. The sexy witchdoctor leapt up and ran for dear life. The little game was over.

It took me a while after grandma told me to remember my dreams for it to sink in. The metaphysical boggles my mind.

"The dreams were to make me need him." I whispered to myself.

"Exactly!" Grandma confirmed.

"And in my need, he will enslave me."

"Precisely! In this world of ours, you shouldn't need anyone when you're a witchdoctor."

"What now grandma?" I asked in trepidation.

"We get our family back." She was resolute. "Time for the altar."

"Can I ask for help from Gushungo?" I didn't have the confidence we could do it by ourselves.

"Not before we kneel in front of our altar and urge the Story Teller to come home. We have more power over him than any of them."

By sunset, our Story Teller was home. Under my own power.

There! I was done. Breaking it down for Mother Nature. If I'd left out anything, it was because I'd forgotten about it.

What now?

"We wait for a few minutes. Stay silent and in your posture."

A small breeze encircled me minutes later. My basement is dank business. Nothing like a sweet clean breeze wafts in. I thought nothing of it at the time, too consumed in my pain as I was.

"It has been accepted." Grandma interpreted the breeze.

Chapter 2

Day 2 - 3:45 am

The stream is my friend whom I've spent countless hours with, grabbing bottles of water or simply talking. It runs next to the trail I walk my dogs on most days. Our trail is a whole little forest by itself stuck in the middle of the ghetto. Its jam-packed full of grown trees, most of them being fruit trees. I've eaten the sweetest plums and sour tiny apples from those trees in the summer. The grass is tall and lush. Bushes are everywhere. I love it.

We're an element-based religion. In the rustle of the leaves, therefore, I can have great conversations with my ancestors. We bond, something very precious to the Chosen. The stream however is my absolute favorite. I often sit on the rocks beside it, chilling. Water is peaceful. It's hard for me to find peace because of my metaphysical scientist thing. I cherish it when I do. Just being is difficult because it is rare for my brain to come to a standstill. Not when I'm sitting by the stream though. On most days the water is crystal clear. I can see the little multi coloured fish making their way leisurely and playfully up the stream, nature at its most natural and best. Watching the fish is very cathartic.

Moreover, water talks. As it is moved by the breeze, it sends out messages of strength, hope, rejuvenation. There's nothing I need more on a regular basis. When I'm all out of steam, I run to the stream.

Furthermore, water also has another metaphysical purpose. It amplifies things and is the closest to the veil. It is no wonder my son's father chose to accost me by the stream one afternoon.

I took a bottle of wine, music and my dogs to the rocks. I can't afford vacations. If I could, I'd always be gone. No matter. The stream is as good as a trip to Jamaica.

I gratefully sat on the rocks, removed my headphones and turned off the music. I breathed out, feeling some of the tension dissipate from my soul. Who needed a million dollars when Mother Nature birthed such sanctuaries?

The sounds of nature serenaded me so much I forgot to drink the alcohol. When I came to, I decided to offer it to the ancestors who ruled the waters. I opened the bottle.

"To those who bring life, love and beauty. Those who enjoy sparkling things." I poured the wine into the stream as I spoke. "Enjoy! From your daughter Isobel."

It felt right. Life was beautiful.

"Life is beautiful," Mark agreed from beside me. "I never thought I would miss the sun as much as I do."

I went still. My bliss was broken.

"I'm sorry," he apologized. "I didn't know what I was doing to you. I saw you as someone I was fighting. I had to win at all costs. I didn't know you were afraid of me."

I let him say his peace.

"I never knew you," he lamented, "until I got here. I did horrible things to you. I see it now."

He did do atrocious things to me. He pointed guns at my head, threatening me. On one occasion, he encouraged one of his employees to do it. He locked me in our bedroom for as long as a week because I wouldn't sleep with his friends while he watched. Mark brought his other women to the house and kept some of their photographs on the mantlepiece of our formal living room. Sometimes, he had sex with them in our bed and they stole our pillows and comforters. When I couldn't work because I'd just given birth and needed to stay home with our son, he kept me penniless. If I wanted even a single banana, I had to ask him for it. For real, he bought exactly one banana. The man was loaded. The financial abuse was purposeful.

I knew what he was, yet I wanted him with everything in me. He was the love of my life. I forgave him when he broke our engagement twice and cancelled our wedding three times.

Grandma was later to tell me it was the fate of female witchdoctors to get very difficult men. Almost all of us are divorced.

"Light attracts darkness," she said.

Eventually, one day, furious I once again refused to let his friends fuck me for his entertainment, he threw me out of the house. I left with our baby and two garbage bags full of clothes. I was a foreigner in his country. Due to him isolating me, his friends were also the only friends I had. They wouldn't have anything to do with me after I was no longer his. I had nowhere to go and no money. My family wasn't about to hear I needed help.

"You chose a foreigner. Deal with the consequences," were their statements over and over.

How had I ended up homeless, I asked myself when I lay on a park bench, baby in my arms. It was because I'd asked for it, I decided.

I'd spent a whole week locked in the bedroom without food. On the final night of my imprisonment, I fell to my knees in despair, wailing.

"Do something!" I screamed at no one and nothing. "Do something!"

At the time, my mother was actively suppressing my ancestors, yet somehow, they got through to me while I wept in desolation. I didn't think anything of the change in atmosphere. A breeze wafted around me all of a sudden.

"Ask us again," a soft voice whispered in the room.

"Please do something! Anything at all," I begged, not caring who I was talking to. I was in despair. If only I'd been more specific.

The next morning, Mark threw me out with two garbage bags of clothes. It was the last time I saw him. Until he transcended from cancer years later.

"I wasn't aware you were afraid of me," he continued his one-sided conversation at the stream.

He wanted my forgiveness. I wondered about his religion. He wasn't a Christian when he lived. His was a dark faith. He told me he worshipped the devil, as his family had done since slavery a couple of weeks after I moved in with him. Apparently, his great grandfather joined the church. It made them a very wealthy family over the decades. As a teen, he was devout. He went through all the initiations and participated aggressively. He shared experiences of his metaphysical power when he'd been a true disciple.

"I could move water," he told a disbelieving me. "Honestly, I made waves. Then the whole thing got too dark. I bailed due to the influence of my brothers."

Beside our bed was his "bible." He encouraged me to read it. I wouldn't even open it. It had an intimidatingly dark energy I didn't want to get involved in.

I had no problem with Mark's former religion. At least he made it sound like it was all in the past. The signs on the ground proved it. His "church" elders were constantly coming to the house. They would meet in the basement and leave as quietly as they came. He explained they were unhappy with him. He wasn't employing the devout at his company, something he was supposed to do because his great grandfather wrote it in blood.

"I'm over it," he complained. "Keith warned me when I was a teenager this would happen. I wish I'd listened."

Keith was his older brother who not only broke free from the family religion, but also became a pastor. I felt safe in knowing it was all behind him. It took a couple of years for me to realize he lied.

Although he might not have been an active member, he was still a devout. By that time, our fourteen-year relationship was over. I don't know who he worshipped when he died. I stopped talking to him the day he threw my son and I out. In fact, I made it impossible for him to ever find me. Along with my ancestors who came on full force live after they rescued me, we built a metaphysical wall between him and I.

My ancestors said he was never going to be satisfied until I was dead. Therefore, I was never going to see him again. It was hard, for I still loved him. Regardless of his plans for me.

Unfortunately for me, the spiritual zip code he lived under before his death, was keeping him on this physical plane by force. I saw him more now than when I lived with him. What a bummer! On every occasion, he apologized to me for what he'd put me through. I figured he needed to apologize to everyone he wronged and set things right before they let him move onto the next level.

Purgatory was as close as I could get in my mind although, I haven't yet seen or heard of Christianity's purgatory in the veil. The Christians I've seen transcend either go at once, or wait for thirty days to be collected. Those who remain for thirty days, (I've counted the days) don't talk to anyone. They go about their business, until they're no longer there. It's all very civilized.

"I'm sorry," he said again.

I stood up and left. I was bound to see him again and hear the same speech. He'd already given it to me lots of times, in my bedroom, bathroom, supermarket, when I was getting an oil change and at the mall.

I couldn't give him what I didn't have to offer. My religion is specific. There are some things which are done to us that hurt the soul to the point of no return. When such a thing occurs, it isn't up to the individual to absolve the perpetrator. It is up to God. As his daughter, I laid my pain at God's feet. I asked Him to give forgiveness on my behalf to those I couldn't exonerate.

The only person I ever forgave was my dad. I loved him, despite what he did to me.

Mark's forgiveness was only going to come from the God of Light, the God of all things, the Creator, He whose DNA I carry. At this rate, he was going to keep me company for the rest of my life.

I hadn't visited the stream since the encounter with my ex. It certainly never crossed my mind I would be stumbling in the dark, at three forty-five am, in a bid to get to the stream so as to fulfill Mother Nature's dues.

She asked for water from an active stream and fine grains of soil found underneath the same water in exchange for safe passage in her air and oceans. We required permission to launch Musa's missiles back at him. It was a request that was required to return Musa's weapons to him.

Walking the trail leading to the stream in the dark frightened me to an extreme. I felt myself shamelessly trembling uncontrollably. The flashlight wobbled in my nervous hand. I erratically beamed the light everywhere, especially the ground I was walking on. I was looking for snakes, my greatest fear. There were snakes on this trail. I'd met them, in broad daylight while I was minding my own business.

I was deathly afraid of snakes. When I was seven, I was bitten by a poisonous snake at my grandfather's farm. It was such a tiny little thing. I didn't see it until it was wriggling away. The deed was done. The searing pain, however, was immediate. It took a long time for anyone to pay attention to my pain. I can't blame my grandparents. They were in charge of more than seventeen grandchildren. It was probably hard to keep up with our goings on.

A little more than an hour later, my bawling finally made them take notice. They called my father. This was easier said than done. There were no phones available within a ten mile radius. One of the cow hands ran to the nearest store for the phone. Hunting for the shopkeeper further delayed the help.

The deed was eventually done. My dad drove for three hours from the city, using little dirt roads where cars sometimes got stuck in the mud during the rainy season. At times, debris and fallen trees cut off the road, which meant the driver had to get out of their car, clear the debris then keep it moving. As it was late and pitch black, it made my dad's job much harder. My dad took me to the nearest clinic, an amazing place about a couple of hours away from the farm, using the same dirt roads.

What followed was the most excruciating experience of my life.

The male nurse was pretty impressed I was still in good shape. He didn't dwell on the fact that I didn't know what kind of snake bit me. I described it as much as I could. He went with it.

There was no anti venom available. In times of need, it was flown from South Africa. I was a little black girl in segregated Rhodesia. No one was sending a plane for anti- venom for me.

This didn't faze the nursing staff. They gushed, instead, about how lucky I was the snake bit me below the ankle. They threw in anecdotes of all the people from the surrounding village who died of snake bites because they were bit either in the abdomen or thigh.

"You're lucky," the nurse was jovial. "The venom hasn't reached any place we can't handle. Don't worry. You'll soon be playing with your friends, even if it's with one leg."

The nursing staff guessed the venom hadn't yet reached my hip. They did this by gauging my screams. It might have been venom to them, but it was fire to me. I felt like I was being burned alive.

"This is nothing!" the nurse continued happily. "Good news! We've decided the venom hasn't gone past your hip. If we're wrong, there'll be a funeral tomorrow."

The nursing staff went into African medicine mode. Without anaesthetics, they cut into my flesh, chasing the venom. I screamed until I passed out. They didn't give a shit. Saving me was more important. I regained consciousness, only to feel the indescribable pain and wished I was unconscious. By the time they finished slicing off bits of poisoned flesh and flushing my blood out of my body by literally cutting off blood vessels which connected my leg to the rest of my body, I'd given in to the pain. We were besties.

All the staff had in hand were mere scalpels and their brains. Africans are the most inventive people when it really counts. They tore my leg apart, got the venom out as much as they could and then sewed me back together. My leg was in a cast for months after. Yes. I FEAR snakes.

Unfortunately for me, there were snakes on the trail. The trail billboard stated it. And, I'd met a few, while taking my dogs on walks. So, taking any of the little beaten tracks in darkness, surrounded by thick foliage was number three thousand on my to do list.

Worse, the trail was at nature's best. There'd been a lot of rain in the last few months. The foliage was thick, the ground dank and fertile. Everywhere was dark and dense because there was no light from the sky. I have a cowardly gene. I inherited it from my father. It had me trembling incessantly at the thought of being bitten by a snake.

Hope flared in the idea of bunnies being eaten by the snakes during the day. They, therefore, couldn't be hunting this early in the morning. I took steady steps forward until I decided the bunnies were clever and had run away escaping the dinner thing. I stopped, intent on retracing my footsteps back to the safety of my car.

"Hurry!" Grandma urged. "Nothing is going to get you."

She was wrong. She'd been dead a long time. No creepy, crawly, poisonous things were ever going to get her. I'd rather be killed by a lion than be bitten by a snake again. They were evil.

"There's nothing evil on earth. Snakes are used by the ancestors to reach out to their conduits. They're good messengers."

Did she mean to say the ancestors, herself included, had me bitten by a snake?

"No," she protested. "It was your destiny. Fight the fear. Fear is the dark side's weapon. It keeps us in chains."

Interesting. Gushungo said the same thing to a client while I was listening.

"Fear is the Devil's weapon. He uses it to keep us in chains. Get rid of the fear!" he yelled at the man. He'd been contemptuous. "Look fear in the eye and dare it."

If only I could. I was cowering, unable to go further.

"I'm with you," grandma promised.

When she said it, I felt the warmth of her hug. Her energy seemed to wrap itself around me. I relaxed. I really wasn't alone. Bottle in hand, more confident than before, I clambered on ahead towards the stream. In the dark, I made out a little wave, not an easy task for a short-sighted girl like me. Relieved and thankful to have found it quickly, I filled my bottle. Now came the hard part. Digging with my fingers for some fine grains under the water. To do so, I had to step into the stream in my sandaled feet.

Fear! It reared its ugly head again. What if there were little horrible, flesh eating things in the water? Dangers were everywhere. It didn't matter that I'd never seen one before in this particular stream. Today was a special day. Anything could happen. I paused for a moment.

"The fine grains of soil?"

There was no getting out of it. I stepped into the water. It was cold, freezing almost. Gasping and eager to leave, I frenetically dug in with my fingers, only to hit tiny stones, weathered by water. I dug deeper. Same thing. Terror gripped me even more. I needed to get out of here. There were snakes, or worse, homeless murderers lurking about.

"It's all stones," I informed grandma frantically.

"Keep digging."

Jesu Christu who is someone's ancestor, what the fuck? Nonetheless, I obeyed. I pushed little stones away from my target area. Nothing.

"Stones," I said again.

"Take the smallest. We need to go."

There is a God up above! I stood up in relief, small stones in hand and ran all the way back to my car with the sounds of little critters and nocturnal animals harassing me!

I literally fell on the mat at my altar in relief. First task completed. I wasn't going to chant alone this time. Grandma and I were going to share my body. She and I would speak as one. I call it semi possession, because I would be cognisant all the way. There are times when one of my ancestors fully embodies me and my energy stands aside. It's happened to me in times of great distress. On those occasions, it felt like I was watching a movie, I'd been removed from the main actor position to audience member.

The longest possession I could remember lasted an hour. It's hard to explain in detail because each possession is unique. The one hour one had me fully conscious, yet, not in charge of my body. It was like I was existing in two timelines or two realities. I couldn't grasp either one. It was freaky. Semi possession was way better. It was a heady thing. I felt stronger, more energetic, amped a thousand times. It also brought me closer to my grandma.

Together we chanted over the water and rocks. "Water is life. Water is death. Oh Great oceans, please accept our dues as directed by your Mother. Allow us to pass so we can fight our battle. We have never sullied your waters with evil. Nor have we harmed the air. Please let us pass."

We repeated it four times before we stopped to wait for a reply. For me, it is the most unnerving time. If I didn't get the water from a place where the oceans approved or if they refused the tiny rocks instead of the fine soil they demanded, we were fucked. I would've to go back and do it again the next morning. There have been times when I've repeated the same ritual many times before it was acknowledged. Those days, it seemed, were gone. I was no longer a novice.

"Our petition has been accepted."

We weren't done. We got permission from Water and air, we now needed earth and fire's approval. I waited patiently for grandma, who disengaged from me, to consult with my other ancestors. They had Mother Nature's list of what she wanted for her children.

"We need you to gather soil, leaves and grass. Take it from the South East. We have to pay our dues to the earth."

This one was easy. I dashed to my front yard, phone in hand. I needed it for the compass. Earth's directions are extremely important. To the East is where all good things come, for the sun rises in the East. The West is where all bad things originate. Its where the sun sets. The North is the battleground of the damned while the South is our home. Those of us who stand for light, begin our struggle in the South. Odd, isn't it? The North is higher up, the South is down there. Is it God's way of saying the good often find themselves under the dominance of the bad?

I found my South East using modern technology easily. I dug out soil, pulled out grass and robbed my little tree of its leaves. Job done.

Earth accepted our offering. Of all the elements, earth was my favorite when it came to offerings. This grand old baby of Mother Nature wasn't fussy. Since earth and fire went together in the same way water and wind did, we were done. We could get on with launching missiles.

"I had no doubt our offerings would be accepted" grandma was pleased. She ululated, to my pleasure. "We're dragons. We own the soil, water, air and fire."

I'd been told this by many witchdoctors. They said I was an apex witchdoctor because I could work with all four elements. We were apparently one percent of the population of witchdoctors in the Bantu territories. I'd never met another.

I assumed they encountered their end before they could harness all four elements because I was on the wanted list of many.

"Tomorrow we light the candle."

The lighting of the red candle was the beginning of the war. I was ready. I felt my power. All along, it had been inside me, untapped. It immediately consumed me, making me feel invincible. Musa didn't know who I was. Too bad for him, he was going to know me. He thought he was the baddest of them all. He was wrong. My mother was. And she taught me well.

Chapter 3

My Mother

Her nickname was Chairman Mao, after the communist China founder. It suited her. Chairman Mao believes she's the only human being in the world. Everybody else is simply an energy source she uses to control her part of the world. The Bantu dark side is about using a person's energy, their very life source.

Their ancestors are from the Right, the hell of our religion. They don't come as ancestors. They come as "shavi." Shavi are an inferior, dark energy, which possesses an individual permanently. The closest you can come to an explanation is by calling it a demon. Only, this Shavi used to be a cruel or evil person when they lived. They went to the Right and were recycled by the dark side onto its progeny, always with a like-minded personality.

Usually maternal, they can't be seen except on exceptional circumstances. They can most definitely be heard. I've talked to many. They are also felt. Dark ancestors have the power to move physical entities. They can shake you or your car, break your plates, cut, punch, kick and make you bleed. It's all happened to me.

They can't be seen because unlike the Light ancestors who walk next to you, they reside permanently inside their conduits. They become part of their souls. You can't tell them apart. You know they're in there from the gleam of their conduits' eyes. It's diamond hard, hot and red. It pops up randomly, then disappears, as if it never existed. You need to know what you're looking for to catch it.

The Bantu dark side practitioners are well endowed with amazing gifts. They can bend time, walk through walls, fly, cover great distances in one step and hover above you while you sleep. They're also very good scientists who upgrade their skills with their absolute devotion to the craft. For instance, the era of zombies is long over for them. Such a backward thing.

Molly's use of zombies showed she was a witchdoctor gravitating to the dark side. She wasn't yet one of them because she used old tools to get her evil work done.

Instead of zombies, the dark side has found a way of enslaving your energy, zombifying it in fact, while you physically carry on.

What happens when someone steals your soul?

These are the metaphysical symptoms of being harnessed.

- Your life doesn't change. Not even in a single way. You remain exactly where you were the moment you were harnessed.

- People begin to hate you suddenly. You can't go anywhere without people aggravating you, even when you've done nothing to deserve it.

- Friends disappear and making new ones becomes extremely difficult.

- Difficulty in finding employment. Not even at McDonald's.

- You can't keep a job, no matter what. It's always you who gets fired, even if you're in the right.

- You can't keep a man or a woman. They will drift in and out of your life, leaving you with babies and bills without a concrete reason as to why they're doing it.

- It can get so bad you won't even get asked out by anyone. You go without a partner for years. There's a reason why. Sex in the metaphysical brings money in the physical. If you're not having sex, it means you're not getting to your metaphysical wealth. This means the wealth is going to someone else. Your slave- master.

- Blocked opportunities. (A major one for me because they blocked everything in my life. Some of it is still blocked.)

- Your prayers don't reach God. How can they? You're in a cage.

The physical symptoms of being harnessed.

- You suffer mentally from various ailments, depression, hallucinations, and various disconnections from society.
- You're so exhausted on the daily you can't get out of bed. When you do, you need energy boosters. You're out there searching for seaweed to give you some mojo.
- Constant headaches and dizziness.
- You could lose time, literally.
- Extreme forgetfulness.
- You can't sleep. You end up visiting the doctor, asking for sleeping pills. Still, you're as awake as an owl while everyone else is sleeping.
- You gain weight. You haven't changed your diet, yet, you keep getting bigger. You go on a diet, and you barely lose any weight.
- Your hair thins and falls out. Where it falls from, it doesn't grow back normally. It takes more than six months for you to have even a small fuzz of hair.
- You catch random, unexplained by science illnesses.
- A constant ringing in the ears, most especially, one ear.
- You become clumsy. You trip and fall in the weirdest places.
- You break things, especially glasses and plates.

The result of this grief is self-destruction, either through alcohol, drugs, committing a crime or suicide.

You know the feeling! The one where you feel trapped in your life. No matter what choice you make, it ends up in disaster. You know those days! When you crumble on the carpet, after having worked hard, yet nothing changes. You start a business, work eighteen-hour days, yet, remain poor. You get jobs, and then still can't make ends meet.

Meanwhile, everyone around you is making great progress, moving on with their lives, becoming financially stable. You torture yourself. Asking what are you doing wrong? It becomes the common tune in your head. The hole gets deeper. The world becomes dark for you. You try harder, to no avail. You let go of your values and principles in the hope of winning. Nope!

Bitterness sets in. Hurt comes right along with it.

If you unexpectedly transcend, a great possibility, people say, "she had great potential. We don't know what happened."

That's it right there! You were enslaved in the metaphysical and died a slave.

A slave master can be anyone. In my case, it was my extended family, working en mass. It can be your best friend, your mother or dad. Your boyfriend. They use your energy to enrich themselves.

Think hard. There's always a pattern in your life if you study it. Grandma and I call it following the string. There are people in your life who seem extraordinarily lucky. There are also those who love to put you down. Yet, they've come from where you are. Why is it important to them for you think less of yourself?

The biggest crime in the metaphysical is the stealing of one's metaphysical wealth. They can't do it before they enslave your soul and break you down. The weaker you are physically, the easier it is for them to reap from you.

In our Bantu culture, the dark side especially favors children and young adults as slaves. They're vital, their energy is bright and strong. The dark side's very picky. They go for the ambitious. Those with potential to change the world. They harness their energies and leave behind empty shells. This business explains Africa's inability to rise economically. Grandma says until we stop eating each other, we shall be at the bottom of the barrel.

Chairman Mao, aptly named by her brother Absalom, her sisters Juliet and Roseline are dark practitioners of great note. Theirs is a legacy passed onto them by their mother, who learned from her mother. It goes way back in their family tree.

My mother never missed a day of chanting to her god. She started at eight pm and chanted for a couple of hours every day. She followed this up by another hour of chanting at five in the morning. She loudly chanted in tongues. The whole house reverberated with the sound of her voice.

Sometimes, she implored Jesus Christ. I don't know what that was about. I'm still working it out. She screamed, cried, broke down in ecstasy and was a painful irritant to her family who were trying to get some sleep.

We fought with her often about her noise. She only got louder. As we became older, two of my sisters, Linda and Rumbi joined her. They were regular as clockwork. When her sisters came to visit, the tongue fest was in earnest.

My aunt Juliet, her sons and daughter, my aunt Roseline, my sisters Linda and Rumbi and my mother would get on their knees, face the west and get on with their business of bringing our house down for hours.

Once again, they screamed, "Jesus! Jesus!" every few minutes or so.

They lost control, threw themselves on the floor, writhed while screaming in tongues and yelling about Jesus. There were tears, arms flailing in the air, eyes red, energy strong and cruel.

I was impressed with their devotion to God. Yet I puzzled over the red eyes and energy they produced. I used to ask myself if they were really talking to God.

"No," a voice said in my head. "Move away from them."

This made me even more confused. If they weren't talking to God, who were they talking to? It had to be God. But, why did he make them this way?

Every Sunday the same group ran to church and stayed there the whole day. My tete Retina was later to tell me, after my ascension about the importance of church to the dark skilled.

"When the white man brought his Christianity to us, all the dark skilled practitioners found an umbrella to hide under. They were the first to get to those churches. They commandeered them in the name of devotion to a Christian God. There's no one but dark skilled practitioners in our churches. Even the Reverends, Pastors and so on. They all serve the dark. By the time the good people found this Christian God, it was too late. The dark were in charge. Nothing has changed since then."

Clearly, my mother's coven had it down pat. Juliet is a reverend of the Methodist church. She stands in front of a pulpit every Sunday, teaching people about hellfire. The irony of it all. She produces more hellfire than the devil himself.

On my last visit to Zimbabwe, I noticed some churches had stopped pretending. The dark skilled practitioners were actively advertising their services. It has become the thing. I mean, why not? The country now belongs to them.

"We can make that man regret he dumped you," they posted. "For $55.00, our ancestors will bring him hellfire. Come to church."

Their services are in great demand. It no longer surprises me why my mother lives in church.

My mother and her sisters inherited their dark maternal ancestors, just as my siblings and cousins. Dark practitioners come to light at the age of seven. According to my mother, who is an expert, when a dark spirit chooses a child, the child exhibits certain characteristics. The one they all vow by is a strange kind of sleep walking. It is strange because the sleepwalker doesn't go anywhere. They wake up, walk to the nearest wall and lean against it, fast asleep. The child's training begins right away. They're trained in the dark arts from the age of seven, since it's the age when they sleepwalk to a wall and lean against it.

The dark arts don't play, unlike our side. They plunge the child into an intense course which sees them graduating at sixteen.

While dark ancestors choose their conduits, they can also be given conduits. In other words, a person can choose to serve them. Many do. The ones who choose it, are also immediately indoctrinated with an efficiency they possess from a thousand years.

Their ranks continue to soar, as more people prefer them to the Light. Many of these people are witchdoctors. Molly and Nyanzira decided to go to bat for the dark side. That team was more financially lucrative.

I don't remember my sisters and brother Milton leaning against any wall. But then of course, I hardly lived in my house. It could all have happened, while I was slaving at some relative's place.

It happened that my mother's coven grew from her three sisters alone to her adding in the ranks her three children, Roseline's three and Juliet's five. My cousin Taurai, my aunt Juliet's son is one of the best and heir to their throne. He has embraced the dark side with an unmatched overzealousness. Pity, I didn't know it when he insisted, we were family and should grow closer.

He has a battle on his hands for the throne with my brother Milton. I believe Milton has the most purely evil soul I have ever met. He inherited the "gift" without dilution.

My dad took to warning people about him when he was alive. He told the extended family not to hang around Milton because he was dangerous. Coming from a dark practitioner himself, a very high ranking one at that, it meant my brother executed his business with terrific brilliance.

This is cave in which I was born. Where my mother is, stands the nexus of evil.

When I finally came into my own, they were ready and prepared to unleash their weapons on me. They are a well-organized and ferocious army. There's no retreat or surrender with them. They harnessed my soul for years. When I broke free, they were equipped enough to enslave me again and again. Until I found my awareness. Then it became a never-ending open battle.

The one thing I hate about the dark side is how much they love to toy with their victim. Taurai once said to me in a random conversation, "you know, the family eats one person. The person is a tree with all the fruit. So, everyone plucks the fruit, until the tree can longer produce and is pretty much useless."

I had no idea he was talking about me! He used to tell me all the time he and I were on opposite sides.

"I'm anti progress," he said. "You're for it."

I thought he was talking about modernizing Africa! In my o- pinion, at the time, his words didn't match his actions. He said he was anti progress, yet, he was working on computerizing Zimbab- we's medical system with the government of Zimbabwe's secretary of Health.

I insisted he was for progress too. I figured he was feeling demoralized at the progress of the computerization. I encouraged him to stay in the fight. After all, when he joined the team, they were well on their way to unveiling the program. He had to be pati- ent, I advised. Little did I know he single handedly ended the pro- gram. When he was put in charge of it, he scrapped it and insisted on starting from scratch. It never got off the ground. A year later, they fired him by simply cutting him out of communications.

I noticed a pattern with him from that moment on. Everyth- ing he touched or got involved in turned to dust. I sympathized with him, blamed everyone and everything but him even when I was one of the ones he destroyed. I excused him for destroying my writing career. He took over as my publisher and proceeded to ruin my work. Years of books, stories I'd been given by my ancestors, including the very important "Across the Realm series" went down the drain. I can honestly say I was my cousin's biggest victim and I suffered the most.

If I had studied him from a metaphysical perspective, I would've realized he said his truth. He was anti progress. His job was to stop good things from happening. When progress doesn't happen, people suffer. The dark side flourishes where people suffer, like in my country of birth, Zimbabwe. It is therefore to their benefit to destroy.

I was later to learn Taurai came into his dark skills at the age of seven. His paternal family was so frightened of his power, they did a ritual to bind him.

"We'd never seen anyone so evil," his uncle informed me. "Taurai will finish the whole village and the next!"

These words were imparted as a warning when Taurai decided to cling to me. I should've listened. He not only destroyed my friendships and my career, he almost killed me as well.

According to my ancestors, my mother and Taurai were my greatest enemies. Out of everyone they committed the most deplorable acts. Beating them made me the best.

My story is the same for many female witchdoctors. Had I been a man, my extended family would've revered me. Unfortunately, I was born a girl and they did what my people have been doing for generations. They harnessed me before coming for my life. Out of all the witchdoctors, only ten percent are female in my tribe. The rest were killed. I am a member of a dying breed.

Chapter 4

My first memory of the woman who gave birth to me is when I was four. My adoptive mother, Marita, who was considerably older than her took me to their house for a visit. She lived in the suburbs of Rusape, a small town in the then Rhodesia. Her house must've been magnificent, for very few Africans resided in the neighborhood designated for white people in those days. I don't remember it. I guess I was impressed by the lights, television, massive rooms and even a flushing toilet. My reality was a mud hut in a village.

My elderly parents and I lived in the real back of beyond. The bushes were our toilets. At night, Marita would give me a chamber pot to pee in because it was too dangerous for me to go outside. She was afraid the dark side or some other animals would get me.

She was also very ill. The nights were horrific for us because she was wrecked with coughing and gasping for air. I shared the bedroom with her because her husband, Michael, slept in his own room as was cultural practice for an elderly couple who no longer had sex.

I alone bore witness to her suffering because I lay cuddled in her arms every night. She disengaged from me several times to cough, puke or stumble around the room for air. She hid her anguish well from the neighbors and Michael during the day. She had a reputation to uphold. She was the grande dame of the village. Marita ran the village with an iron fist and a lot of charm. Being ill was not on the menu. She kept her illness well hidden. In the end, it wasn't her illness which took her. It was suicide.

Her love for me was unmatched. She carried me on her back everywhere. We spent a lot of time harvesting worms from trees. Marita cooked them in peanut butter, we ate them for dinner. Our meals were simple because we were poor. Sometimes we had meat or milk with our cornmeal, although it was rare. We got what we could from nature. We ate grasshoppers when they were in season, or field rats, if Michael could catch some.

Villagers also shared food. Whenever someone culled a cow or goat, they would give some to their neighbors. If it was a cow, biltong, dried beef, was also guaranteed. My adoptive parents would also slaughter a cow once a year to share with the neighbors. Those were good times. It meant we could eat our cornmeal with meat every day. The girl who worked for us either made it with tomatoes and onions or with peanut butter.

Watermelon, a fruit I believe should be a vegetable, was the snack of the day, every day. It grew wild in the village. Marita also made a watermelon soup I hadn't eaten watermelon soup since she died until I went to my Tete Retina's for my final transcension.

Tete Retina made it especially for me. It brought back tearful memories.

The best thing Marita made was cornbread. Our oven was the earth itself. Michael dug a hole, where she put pans with cornbread mix in. He covered it with soil and built a fire on top. We ate corn bread for breakfast when Michael sold cotton to the Cotton marketing board. Michael and Marita were subsistence cotton farmers. The cornbread was such a luxury. It put us above everyone else in our village.

The night times were the best for me. Michael was an amazing storyteller. The children from the village and I would sit around a fire, outside where the stars illuminated everything to listen to our traditional fairy tales. Our eyes would go wide and round in entrancement as he unfolded the story of the tortoise, the rabbit, the boy who became addicted to honey. Oh the stories, the songs which were part of the stories and the rhythmic chants made village life.

We munched on peanuts sautéed in nothing but salt and water during Michael's story times. I was happy.

Oddly, seeing how they were so poor, Michael and Marita spoke English to each other, thereby making it my first language. I think they spoke English instead of Shona because Marita went to some Catholic boarding school while Michael was a retired police detective. They felt their superiority in the village.

I know we went to the city for Marita to get medical help. She and Chairman Mao were exceptionally close. As soon as we arrived at the home, Chairman Mao, treated Marita as if royalty had stepped through the door. Although she boasted of a maid and gardener, she choose to prepare our meal herself.

Marita, who was more comfortable with the lesser things in life, chose to sit on the floor in the kitchen, clearly ignoring the kitchen table and comfortable chairs. I sat with her.

I first looked directly at Chairman Mao when she bent over, to place the plates of food in front of us. She was the ugliest woman I'd ever seen. I was later to be told she was the exact opposite by her admirers. She was considered gorgeous. I believe I saw her soul.

The hate within her was so strong it shone brightly in her eyes. There they were, two gleaming, red diamonds. They shot right at me, promising me dire consequences. She hid the malevolence with a smile. I wasn't fooled. Frightened, I ran to hide behind Marita's ample form. I'd never met anyone like her. It rocked my little world.

"What is wrong with you?" Marita chided me. She apologized to Chairman Mao. "My little butterfly isn't usually like this. It must be unfamiliar surroundings."

She tugged at me from behind her. "Come and eat."

The food was a definite upgrade from dried worms and corn meal. Chairman Mao's beef stew was full of tomatoes and onions, unlike ours in the village. The soup was thick and hearty. It was accompanied by a plate of green, sautéed kale. I'd never had it before. The cornmeal itself was whiter and smoother than I'd ever seen. The variety we ate in our village was a dark beige and rough. I should've wanted to dive in. Except, this woman with an energy I'd never encountered had made it.

I refused. I was in danger. I knew it. Marita was embarrassed. She laughed uncomfortably. She wasn't about my behavior.

"You're going to be hungry if you don't eat."

I shook my head vehemently. No way.

"Come on," she became insistent. "Eat."

The firmness in her voice told me she was done with my shenanigans. Still, I stood my ground. Marita was the gentlest soul to me. I knew she wasn't going to spank, nor yell at me. I could do whatever I wanted around her.

"She's spoilt," Chairman Mao's eyes burned with rage. I was transfixed by the emotions she radiated through her eyes. None of them were good. "You should beat her."

Marita laughed as if finally, a joke had entered the room. "This skinny little thing? I would kill her."

Instead my mother dipped her fingers into the cornmeal, made a fist of it and dunked it into the plate of meat. I watched her bring it to her mouth in horror. If she ate, it meant we were staying. She ate it.

"Here," she extended the next cornmeal and relish to me. Because it came from her hand, I ate it. She fed me, bite after bite.

"You treat her like she's something special!" The venom was in the voice was potent. Our eyes clashed. The rage tripled. She could barely control herself. I burrowed into Marita's rolls of fat, in an attempt to get away.

"She's a child." There was definite censure in Marita's voice. It said, "back off!" Chairman Mao accepted it for Marita was older than her. Age matters in Africa. The older you are, the more respect you get.

"Of course," she breathed, uncrossing her legs on the floor as she did so. "She was also born fragile, wasn't she?"

"Indeed." Marita relaxed.

All I could think about then was when we were leaving. I wanted to go. Little did I know at seven years of age, my dad would wrestle the two parents I knew to be mine for custody and I would end up living with Chairman Mao and her children. The week I moved into her house was the one Marita died.

Still puzzled at my new living arrangements, the woman whom I now had to call mother, found me in her palatial home, grabbed me by the shoulders, shook me hard and yelled, "It's your fault she's dead. You killed her! Had you not come; she would still be alive. You're evil. A witch!"

It took years for me to learn the truth of Marita's death. She committed suicide because she couldn't live without me. I guess, in a way, my mother was right.

I carried the label of witch for many years, thinking I deserved it because I killed Marita. My mother doubled on it.

"Look at her feet!" she said to the group of women socializing in our garden as I walked past. "They're just like her grandmother's, her father's mother. They're the feet of a witch! My daughter's a witch and I'm living with her! If I'm still alive by the end of the year, it would be a miracle."

This charge is a death sentence. People were burned at the stake as late as 1980 when accused of witchcraft. Witch burnings were social events, interestingly they were encouraged by the dark side.

It makes sense. Innocent people found themselves at the stake, with the dark side stoking the flames. Teachers, doctors, geologists, anyone at all, found themselves branded and executed within a couple of weeks. As we were in the middle of a civil war, fraternizing with white people also got you killed. Only a witch could like white people, they said. No doubt, they were also selling the independence cause. The freedom fighters, as they called themselves helped in the capture of the so-called witch. It was them who tied the victim to the stake.

Watching a witch burning was as exciting as the Olympics for people. They looked forward to it, took bets on who would be fingered and dressed warmly for the witch burning evenings.

My mother was fingered a year after she tried to get the entire black population to burn me at the stake. She went to a witchdoctor with some of the villagers to put her petition forward because no one was taking her seriously. In the history of witch burnings, it was the first time a witchdoctor had been consulted. Maybe it was because I was a child, and the idea of burning me was too repulsive for the villagers.

A witchdoctor declared her the witch instead. Apparently, the witchdoctor got so frantic when my mother walked into their consulting room, leaving the people without a doubt at her dark skills. My mother ran from the village witchdoctor, didn't wait a single second, packed some clothes, grabbed the dogs, crammed four children into her small Citroen, and we were off in the middle of the night. My dad was away on business. He came home to an empty house.

Funny enough, we didn't live in the village. We lived over the hill, in a suburb where we were the only black people. Our house, nestled at the bottom of the hill, was set on four acres of land. It overlooked the Rusape dam.

Our manicured garden was full of very well-maintained rose bushes. We had a massive swimming pool and an orchard to boot. Yet my mother spent all her time in the village. In the end, it drove her out of her paradise.

Once my mother takes on a campaign, she doesn't stop. Only death parts her from her goals. She took her claim of my dark skills to Harare, our country's capital city where my dad had a house ready for us by the time we got there. This house was also in a similar suburb to the one we left.

Again, she found a village on the outskirts of the city. She wanted us to go to the village school. The school accepted my brother and two sisters and rejected me. The headmaster told her the class was full. I had to attend school at the white children's school in our neighborhood.

My mom took this rejection to their village witchdoctor.

"It's because she's dark skills practitioner," my mom insisted to the witchdoctor.

The witchdoctor laughed it off. "We have one class for each grade. The class is full. By the way, why do you, a nurse whose husband makes a lot of money want to bring your children to a village school? I mean, you have to drive one hour by dirt road to get them here every day. It can't be good for your car. Besides, it doesn't make sense."

It was clear to my mother there would be no witch burning in this village. She took her plight to her extended family. Once, at an extended family function, where there were hundreds of people, she said to her relatives within my earshot, "the child has the most wicked eyes. She was brought onto this earth to ruin people's happiness. She's a witch. She deserves to be burned for everyone's safety."

It was odd how she was always the one who ended up running from the same accusation. When the villagers where my siblings attended school decided she was a dark skills practitioner, she took them out of school and we changed neighborhoods. This time, we were in the heart of upper-class Harare. There were no villages in sight.

Chairman Mao found another way of getting rid of me. She volunteered me to relatives as baby-sitter, fill in maid and sometimes simply forgot to come and pick me up, whereby I would be stuck where I was, unless my dad was in the country.

As the unloved one of her daughters, my relatives put me to good use. During the school holidays I worked eighteen-hour days in Juliet's house as her stand in maid. Due to the harsh working

90

conditions, her hired help always ran away from her. It was a family standing joke for she was known for her unabashed cruelty to humanity. If she wasn't married to such a rich and powerful man, her family would've ostracized her. Fortunately for her my uncle had clout, as the government secretary of Industry and technology. They needed him.

Uncle Chris even discussed his wife's cruelty in bemusement.

"Sometimes I think she's crazy! How can anyone be so unnecessarily cruel?"

Unlike me, he didn't see the two shining red diamonds in her eyes. All he saw was a wife who was obsessed with Jesus and the church. She donated thousands to the church, was a patron of an orphanage and lectured women on how to be a good, obedient, Christian wife. She had the wife thing down. I have to give her that.

I could understand his surprise. Hers was a luxurious lifestyle. She was called the spoiled wife. She got everything she wanted from him, including family vacations to their house in the South of France. She wore nothing but the best silk imported from Asia and jet setted around the world at a whim.

He bought her the house she desired, even though he felt it was too extravagant. My aunt's house was massive, twice as big as ours. It had three major living rooms, a hallway favored by snakes because the architect decided to make an indoor garden, many bedrooms with their own bathrooms and a kitchen area made of several rooms.

At the end of her seven acres were the servants' quarters. Her maids could've enjoyed the luxurious apartments built for them by the former owner, if only she allowed them to live there.

Instead, they slept with me on the cold stone floor of the dining room, despite the many empty, well-furnished bedrooms. We were squeezed between the dining furniture with only one blanket among us. Southern Africa is cold at night. Her neighborhood, being up a hill, was colder, especially with the design of the house. It was created to be more outdoorsy than indoor.

When a new maid was found, I was the one to orient them. I introduced her to going without food or rest for days. I taught her how to polish the stone floor to my aunt's satisfaction. She wanted to see her face in the stone. If she didn't, there was hell to pay. Everything in the house was hand washed because aunt Juliet didn't believe in washing machines. She wanted the blankets and comforters in the entire house washed every three days.

Food was only for the family. We ate dog food after dinner every day except when my uncle was home. When he was home, I ate with the family and the maids also got plates at the same time. Unfortunately, like the one percent of all men in Africa, he was hardly ever home.

At three am, we were to wake up and play with Taurai. He was two years old then and had trouble sleeping. Aunt Juliet wasn't about to leave the comfort of her husband's bed to settle her son. This meant we only got a couple of hours of sleep every day.

"We don't get to sleep here!" Nancy, one of the new maids protested after we finished handwashing a load of blankets. "We don't eat either! Dog food? What the hell!"

"You'll get used to it," said my nine-year old self who'd actually had to work alone in this house many times. I wished for school desperately. At least then I would be free.

"We never stop working," she complained, looking like she was about to pass out from exhaustion. I'd been there many times. I was now well trained. Even though she was a good ten years or so older than me, I knew she wasn't going to last.

"No." What else could I say?

Thank goodness Nancy ran away a couple of days after my servitude was over, otherwise I would've been stuck there longer. The breaks away from her home were welcome for I would always be back, no matter what.

When I became a teenager and weight loss was the thing to do, I told my friends I didn't need to diet because I would soon be at a fat farm, losing whatever pounds I'd gained.

Roseline was better. Her red diamond gleam was less determined too. I actually loved being in her home. A single mother, she married and divorced three times, career driven with an active social life, she barely spent time at home. She was a prominent government official who also traveled a lot, like my dad and uncle. Many of those journeys were taken with uncle Chris. I was later to learn they had a raging affair and a baby to boot, if family gossip is to be believed. Tete Retina also told me years later Roseline knocked boots with my dad as well.

I didn't put it past her because she loved men. She had many of them too, which kept her away from home even when she was in the country. As she wasn't home, I was the lady of the house. At fourteen, I was in charge of everything, including her three children. Those were peaceful, happy days. I was always willing to go to her place.

Living in my own house was a nightmare. The other day my dentist said, "your teeth are all cracked. You must've suffered a lot of violence. Who used to beat you?"

Who didn't beat me? My mother literally set people on me. I couldn't even take a bath in peace. There were many times when I was dragged out of the bathtub, naked and beaten. At her request my brother Milton, who was four years older than me, or one of my mother's brothers would beat me.

There were many bathrooms in our house. I learned to use the only one with a lock. It didn't stop those my mother tasked with disciplining me. They would try to break the door down.

I rarely knew what I'd done to get such a thrashing. At one time, Chairman Mao said I'd took too long using the bathroom because I'd been in there for nine minutes taking a shower.

There were also times when my mother and her sisters jumped me. Not to mention the occasions I dodged beer bottles thrown at me by her. A beer bottle got me one day. It broke my tooth in half and left me with a split lip. Blood gushed everywhere.

I can't forget the time Chairman Mao and her sisters attacked me while I was on the phone with my friend because Rumbi, my older sister by two years, wanted to call her boyfriend. Since I'd just said hello to my bestie Faith, I felt my sister could wait five minutes before she made her call. My mom and her sisters who were visiting disagreed with me. I got my braids and nails pulled out.

When I went to school the next day, Faith had told everybody what happened to me because she'd heard the whole thing. I understand women who suffer from physical abuse and what they go through when the whole world knows your life is far from perfect. They don't want their mess spread about. It's humiliating. We all have an image we protect.

My peaceful place was the toilet. I spent many hours there with my back to the door. To this day, I'm obsessed with toilets. They have to be the best room in my house.

It didn't take long for me to realize I should never have come back to her. When she gave me up, she hid behind our culture. It was only temporary she told my dad. I was refusing to latch to her breast. She was afraid I would starve to death. As she was the wife of a successful lawyer she got away with the excuse.

As I was being given to a family member, my dad acquiesced, not knowing I was meant to be gone forever.

He, however, in his ignorance came to visit me often. He spent his off days in the village with me, Michael and Marita. He gave them money for my upbringing, bought clothes for me and brought groceries on a regular basis. Truth to tell, I don't remember him being there. He took stories of me back to Chairman Mao and they all had to do with my abilities, which by that time had manifested.

"Isobel can tell if there's going to be a clan funeral," he said. "It took me time to work it out. When she cries all night, someone dies. Its guaranteed."

He told Chairman Mao I predicted the outcomes of his court cases accurately. I also warned him about an accident on his motorbike. It happened.

The family went to witchdoctors to find out why I saw things that came to pass. My mom was in front of those spiritual delegations.

"She is Chosen," a witchdoctor declared. "You have to fix her. Do the rituals. She is amazingly powerful."

"No," dad refused. "I don't want that kind of life for my child. She's going to be a writer, an educated woman."

My dad always told me I was going to be a famous writer. He predicted it the day I was born. He put a pen in my hand when I was hours old and declared it to the doctor and nurse who helped at my birth.

"She's going to be a writer!"

Michael also did the same thing. When I was taken from them, he came to visit often. One day, he gave me a set of pencils, "for your writing. You're going to be an amazing writer."

I later learned my dad, being a dark skills practitioner knew about me before I was born. He believed if he encouraged me in my career, I wouldn't pick up the lantern as the one who brings the light into the cave. I would be too busy.

As for Michael, he went to a witchdoctor to find out how I was going to fare, since I'd been taken away from them.

The witchdoctor told my parents and the spiritual delegation I was going to be a writer. It was part of my gifts, so they didn't have to worry.

"She is, however, still the Chosen. Work on it," the witchdoctor insisted. "If you don't, she will suffer. The ancestors will have the one they want. She has amazing gifts. The people need them."

My father hesitated.

"No!" my mother raged. "It's filthy business. We want none of it."

Spiritual delegations came to a halt. Not before my mother took the witchdoctor aside and asked for something to suppress the ancestors. He gave her some herbs. She brought them to the village and force fed me. My mom was extremely unhappy about it. Like all things to do with my people, it became a secret until my aunt, Tete Retina told me in 2017.

The suppression of the ancestors was to continue well into my adult life. It wasn't always herbs. Sometimes it was incisions into my skin. The witchdoctor would cut little slits on my wrists, back, forehead, on top of my head and feet. He would rub herbal concoctions on the bleeding cuts and then I would be sent home.

There were occasions I was taken to rivers, dunked in them til I thought I would drown. And then there were the times I would be dumped, in back of beyond villages, to live with noted witchdoctors at my mother's behest. She was a barracuda at organizing these things.

I have to tell you, no one told me shit. I was a child. I didn't have any rights. In our culture you also don't have the right to any information. As much as my mother tried, something always happened to show her she was failing. It made her more determined.

Once, when I was eight, I was violently woken from a deep sleep. My heart was beating so fast I couldn't breathe. As I sat there, frightened out of my pants, I asked myself what had woken me.

"Hello Isobel," a blonde-haired white male whispered from the direction of my closet.

Oh my God, a ghost! My fear was palpable. I started shaking.

"Don't be afraid." He didn't move. Thin and tall, he was dressed all in white. Light radiated powerfully from him.

No, no, NO! I squeezed my eyes shut, willing him to go away. He was going to kill me. I was sure of it. I crawled to the corner of my bed and covered myself up. I had an idea if I stayed like this for a long time he would go away. I have no idea how long I remained hidden. To me, it was forever. When I finally looked towards my closet again, he was still there.

"I'm not here to harm you Chosen one. I'm here to deliver a message. You must stop your parents from doing these things to you. They're harming you."

I found my courage. I ran out of my bedroom and up the stairs to my parents' room. Grateful my dad was home, I burst in and screamed, "there's a white man in my room!"

My dad, the eternal coward sat up, petrified. "What man? How did he get in? What the hell is the boy at the gate doing, letting people in? It's the middle of the night."

"He says you're harming me," I reported.

"Who said that?" my mother woke up.

"The man! He called me the Chosen one."

My mother nudged my father. "Go and check it out."

"You go!"

My dad wasn't moving. He was sometimes known to hide under the bed in fear of anything.

"You said a white man?" my mother asked.

I nodded.

"What does he look like?"

I described him. My dad relaxed and prepared to go back to sleep. "It was a ghost. We bought this house from white people. They're walking around here doing their rubbish. Go to bed."

Still afraid, I stood stock still. I couldn't go back there. It never crossed my mind to go and sleep in one of my siblings' rooms. What good would it do? I shared a room with my little sister Linda. She slept through the whole thing. He would find me in whatever room I went into, except my parents'. I was safe with them. They had to let me stay. I couldn't ask them though. It's not the way.

My mother got into action. A former nurse, she quickly rummaged through her drug cabinet and came up with a handful of pills.

"Drink them," she supervised.

I gulped them down one by one with the glass of water she passed me.

"Now go to bed."

I turned and left.

The next day, my mother, Juliet and Roseline took me to an old lady who quickly went about slicing my skin with a razor and applying concoctions. The pain was agonizing. It still wasn't comparable to the year I spent in bed at twelve, unable to use my legs from an unknown ailment doctors couldn't get their heads around. The metaphysical always gets physical with time.

My headaches began the day after the witchdoctor cut into me. Sometimes, they were severe. I couldn't see or hear for days. They lasted for longer than thirty years. Temporary blindness and deafness became the norm in my life.

Chapter 5

Day 3 - 3:15 am

The Fire!

"**M**usa, I have declared war on you. In order to defend myself and destroy your plans for me, I need to make you back up and disappear. DISAPPEAR!"

Screaming with a passion is the thing to do when the fire is lit.

"Louder," Grandma wasn't impressed. "More emotion."

"I trusted you! You were supposed to guide and teach me. Not steal from me. Guess what, you're not the first and you won't be the last. At least from now on, when other practitioners raise their spears at me, they will know I am a formidable enemy. I'm going to crush you, so the others will learn."

I was remembering everybody who'd done the same shit to me at this point. The screaming, with tears streaming down my face was very therapeutic.

"I call upon all my ancestors. ALL. OF. YOU! Rise. Fight for your daughter. Fight until the end of time. RISE FROM YOUR GRAVES. RISE FROM YOUR SLUMBER. WE ARE AT WAR. I send all of you in Musa's direction. Teach him you're the oldest. The most revered. The best there is. Tell him he can't mess with your daughter. Show him I am protected. Show him he can't steal one of you and get away with it. Pummel him with truth. He decided to steal one of you. Now he pays."

Catching my breath was getting harder. I was angry, out of my mind.

"Destroy him! Scatter his ancestors into a state of confusion. Let his weapons detonate at his feet. Make him understand there will be no forgiveness. For him, his child, his grandchild, til the end of time."

"Louder!"

"We call upon those who were slaughtered by this man. Rise to take your revenge. Now's your time to make him pay," I chanted. "Remember what he did to you. Fight with us."

Building a coalition was dicey business, at least in my opinion. I preferred working alone, primarily because I hated talking to dead people and other's people's ancestors whom I didn't know. When these energies were in the room, I got freezing cold. I also couldn't trust them. Besides, they scared me.

Nevertheless, my ancestors insisted on building a coalition.

"I call upon the spirits whom Musa imprisoned in order to gain more power. Rise against this man. You have no master. Step forward because we have released you from your chains. Join us."

One never knew what was going to come out of those cages kept by the dark witchdoctors. They kept all sorts of energies in them, from animals with metaphysical power to human souls. Some of that energy was meant to be caged. Yet, I had to trust my ancestors at this point. These Harry Potter times are full of stress and angst.

"One more time."

"Rise," I hollered, hitting my grandma's walking stick on the mat. I was opening the gates of hell with the ritual. "You're free! Musa is a murderer! He killed you. It's time to take your revenge. Rise imprisoned ancestors. You're free! Right the wrongs with the swiftness of the wind."

I said his name over and over, stomping my ceremonial mat with my grandma's walking stick in a rhythm of three beats every few seconds.

"Enough!"

I stopped at once. The atmosphere in the room had somehow changed during my frenzied calling. I hadn't felt it then. I did now. A cold breeze approached from behind me. I shivered.

"Don't look back and don't engage." Grandma was on it.

"You're making noise," a voice whispered in the coldness. The voice was even colder, icy in fact. I shuddered in reaction. This one, wasn't a good dude.

"What should I do?" I asked grandma.

"I'll handle it," she replied. She spoke to the entity. "In what way are we making noise?"

"All this business about wanting to destroy Musa just because he needed your grandchild's light. He was only going to take some of it. Not all of it. Yes. He tried it with your ancestor. But he's back isn't he? Why would you want to destroy him?"

"What do you want?" Grandma wasn't known for her gracious manners.

"Musa will walk away if you destroy the herbs, he gave you for protection. He gave you herbs. He would like you to destroy them because his essence is on them. He can't leave you alone while those herbs are in action."

"All we have to do is get rid of his protection herbs?" Grandma's voice was soft, friendly almost.

"Yes. And he will walk away."

"What did he want in the first place? You said a "little light?" Grandma was practically seductive. I, on the other had was frightened into absolute silence. I didn't move a single muscle. I wanted to disappear. This entity was malevolent, no matter how hard he tried to pretend otherwise.

"He wanted her essence. Her. She was the prize. Her beauty, her energy, sexual energy."

"Of course," my grandma sounded gracious. "He took the Story Teller and gagged me to weaken her defences. I see."

"I'm glad. No harm done. Get rid of his herbs, especially the ones you already used around your house. Dig them out. Throw them away. And Musa will go."

The freezing breeze vacated the room.

"Musa's watching us."

"What?" I asked in a whisper.

"Don't look!" Grandma warned me, "the North is an open portal on your wall. I can see him. He's watching us."

"Has he been spying on us all this time?"

"Yes."

"How?"

"He gave you something. You brought it with you from Zimbabwe. It enables him to spy on you. He sent his servant to stop us from opening his cage."

"What are we going to do?"

"He went to the trouble of sending an emissary. It means we have succeeded in opening his cage. His next best thing is to send you something awful, so you won't be able to turn his slaves against him. His own protection methods are in the way. He needs you to remove them in order to attack you."

I was busy thinking the servant was doing us a favor. It sounded like a great bargain to me. I would get rid of Musa's protection herbs in my yard and house. In return, he would go away. When the servant placed the deal, I sighed with relief. I didn't want to fight.

Grandma blew my hopes right out of the water and into the universe.

"Now what?"

"First, we're going to close the portal he's using to spy on us. Second, we're going to reprogram his protection herbs in order to take away his incantations and replace them with ours. The herbs belong to us. We paid for them. The realm of the ancestors acknowledges this. Afterward, we're going to turn his slaves against him."

Chapter 6

Musa

Musa was my least favorite chosen elder, from the moment I saw his picture. It was quite an innocent picture. The image was of a family man in his late forties. He was wearing a karate uniform along with shaven head. He was in a regal pose, hands proprietarily on his son's shoulders. The son appeared to be a preteen, cute and also in a Karate uniform. While Musa was a black belt, his son was a yellow.

Musa exuded modernity, education, somberness and dignity. There was nothing to hate, nor distrust from the image. Yet, all the while he professed to be a harmless, very professional witchdoctor of the Light, his energy defied him. It said he was dark, greedy, cruel even.

"You've got to go. He teaches protection, something you need. You can't live in this metaphysical world without the ability to protect yourself," my grandma insisted.

"There's no one else?" I asked.

Surely ZINATHA had other protection witchdoctors in their rank whom they could give me. Not only did he make me uncomfortable, he also lived an hour and a half away from my village. Gas was non-existent. My cousin already told me it would be difficult to go long distances because the country had no fuel.

"At the very least, you will learn something." Grandma wasn't giving up. "We're only as good as you. In order for us to work in this world, we take information from your head. This is a fine opportunity for you to learn. This man does one thing in a very spectacular fashion. Protection. You're going."

The thing was, I found him very pushy. I didn't like it. It took me years to get out from under my mother and her extremely controlling ways. I was therefore allergic to being told what to do.

While still in Canada, Musa insisted I stay with him for a few days before heading to my village. He brought it up several times.

"No," I explained. "I have a whole lot of other rituals ahead of yours. I will see you the second week I'm in Zim."

"Your people hate you. Let me protect you before you step foot in their domain."

I was aware of their animosity. It meant nothing. I had to get my transcension done. Period. Besides, Tete Retina was looking forward to seeing me, despite all the others. No doubt, they were all going to pretend to adore me. They were going to gush about how much they missed me, hug and love on me and shit. It was the way of the people. I could deal.

"Grandma has decided we're going straight to the village," I was firm. "She says I can only learn from anything they choose to throw my way."

"Well, let me just say, don't eat anything you're given by any-one."

That was a common warning. I'd been receiving it since I was a child.

"Serve your own food. If someone brings you a plate of food, give it to a child. Make it look like a joke, nevertheless, give it to a child."

"Thank you," I heeded his words in respect. At the time I felt terrible. Here I was, hating on him and he was doing nothing but trying to protect me.

When I got to the village a couple of weeks later, my instinct to cancel him and ask for another protection master was stronger. He called too many times, wanting me to set an exact date and time, for me to be comfortable with the whole thing. Witchdoctors are not allowed by metaphysical law to chase clients. Clients are suppo-sed to come under their own power. The right to choose governs our religion to the very end. Yet, here he was pursuing me, running me to ground every ten hours or so. He sent me WhatsApp messages asking to talk.

As difficult and expensive as it was to make a call of any kind in Zimbabwe, I called. His one question was always, "When are you coming?"

I was beginning to lose my patience. My ancestors approved of him still. Grandma said he had something we needed. I respectfully allowed him to annoy me. I decided his personality rubbed me the wrong way. It couldn't be because he was a dark witchdoctor masquerading as a light one. He was simply aggravating as a person. I could deal.

He totally bothered me on the hour, every hour the morning I left to do his rituals. I went with my cousins Wes and Greg.

"What hotel are you staying at?" he asked when we entered his city, Kadoma.

"Like none of your business!" I finally snapped.

He was taken aback. Perhaps because I was a woman. I enjoyed shocking him. It was time he knew I didn't play the weak, culturally respectful woman. Neither did I beat about the bush. I'm the granddaughter of a very rare spirit to our people. A feminist. My grandma died defending her freedom. I don't get controlled by men. I don't bow down either. I may be African, but I draw the line at some things to do with male and female interaction. I was never going to "take my place" beneath the "wisdom" of a man. First off, men weren't any wiser than women. Furthermore, I'd never had a man take care of me. Not even my dad. I was his least favorite daughter.

There was a time when I asked him why he fought my adoption. In my opinion I should've been left with my first parents. They loved me.

He said, "your adoptive parents were poor. I'm rich. I couldn't let you live there while your siblings had it all."

He obviously changed his mind in time. While my siblings received private school education all the way, I forced my parents to send me to a private school the last two years of high school. He found my siblings universities of their choice out of the country, even offering my brother Harvard. Milton turned it down, to his disappointment. When it came to me however, he looked me in the eye and asked, "What are you gonna do with your life? You better find something affordable and close to home."

I wanted to go to Wesleyan college in the USA. I saw their brochure and fell in love. I would study writing, for I'd won every national award in writing Zimbabwe had. The college was also courting me heavily.

When my dad said those words to me, I forgot about Wesleyan and my dream of being free of Zimbabwe and my family. I went to college for Mass Communications.

Pity the oppression didn't end with my dad. I learned when a man was in control of my life, I had to curtail my dreams. I was therefore very angry with Musa dogging me, wanting to know the hotel I was staying at. No doubt, he picked one close to him.

"We will see you when we see you!" I cut the phone.

My cousins and I decided to stay at a safari lodge out of town. This decision was to bother Musa during the entirety of the rituals. He wanted us to change hotels, stay close to him. We stood our ground. I was even more annoyed than ever. He attempted to exude concern. I saw it as fake.

We met Musa in the late afternoon. My first opinion of him was he was weird. After I checked out the massive house he was building, I also realized he was not only expensive, he was also too power hungry. The scent of hunger for control and wealth was everywhere in his house.

What kind of witchdoctor of light was this? Usually, witchdoctors of light are surrounded by a lot of people. Their houses are busy and noisy. They hold the true courts of the Bantus, for they tell your fortune in front of everyone and no one gives a fuck. They do communal healings because they have no time to heal one person at a time. They're worked off their feet. True rock stars. For little money. Nor do they care about it.

Gushungo was a witchdoctor of light. His life was chaotic. He had clients sleep over, refusing to leave. He lectured, healed and ran away when it became too much.

Musa's place said, "no one comes here unless if they have to."

Hmmm.

"Stay," grandma commanded.

If I couldn't trust myself, I could at least trust my ancestors. He took me into his consultation room and opened the court of the Bantu. Musa is from Malawi, another African country. His Hakata, (divination tools) were oblong pieces of dark wood. They were huge and clumsy. Very different from the Hakata used by my people. We use shells. Some add ivory shaped in the form of bones. Since using ivory was outlawed a long time ago, those who still use them inherited them from witchdoctor relatives who once lived. Divination stones are also popular. There are witchdoctors who read you from a bowl of water, others who use tobacco in a plate, and even more who don't use tools at all. They simply sit back and tell you what is.

I can do that too. I'm very good at it. I don't need Hakata to "see." I use Hakata when the person isn't in front of me. When they are, I don't need my shells.

Musa's Hakata were quite unique. He gave them to me to hold in my hand. Another difference. I was the one who threw them on his board. He read them. I read along.

"Are you reading with me?" he wasn't pleased.

I shook my head, lying. "I bow to your ancestors and their expertise."

He discussed my health in detail. I saw my life was undoubtedly heading in the right direction, the bad direction. I was stuck in my past. Progress was zero. Very disappointing. I thought I'd grown in the metaphysical. Clearly, I still had a lot of work to do.

He talked about my headaches.

I saw I still had a lot of enemies. How the hell was I gonna banish these motherfuckers?

He mentioned the brilliance and strength of my ancestors, while pointing out if it were not for them, he would've refused to see me.

The irony of it all ladies and gentlemen, I was thinking, from the way the Hakata was placed, I shouldn't have come. I couldn't make out his ancestor. I felt an energy which wasn't the same as an ancestral energy. It was inferior to ancestral energy, more muted. It seemed to have a strength it kept leashed during the reading. How odd. My ancestors were at their strongest and brightest when I gave readings. So were every other witchdoctor's. They practically sizzle.

Musa's ancestral energy puzzled me. I excused it by saying his ancestors were a different Bantu. Who knew how they did things in Malawi? Certainly not me.

Halfway through the reading however, I got the feeling Musa was using my ancestors to give the reading, and not his. I shrugged it off. It was well known that my ancestors were the best at the business of reading a soul. Perhaps Musa's ancestor needed help. In my opinion, he certainly did. His was a weak ass reading. The worst I'd had in fact.

What really got my goat was his incessant complaining. He criticized me for coming late. I thought we came on time.

"I want to take you to the river for a deep cleansing. It's almost dark," he moaned.

"There's plenty of time," I replied.

"I think we should do whatever we can and finish off the rest tomorrow morning," he suggested.

Oh, hell no! I wasn't coming back to his court for another day.

"No," I shook my head. "I'm leaving for my village tomorrow morning. First thing."

"If you changed hotels and use the one closer to me, we can get it done before you leave."

"I want to stay at the safari lodge. I need to wake up to animals." Now, I was more grateful than ever we chose the safari lodge. It was a good forty-five kilometers away from Musa's house. The more distance between us the better.

He wasn't pleased.

"Your transcension ritual is long. We may not be able to finish."

"Do what you can." There was no changing my mind. I couldn't care less if I didn't finish the ritual. I was tired of rituals. I'd been through nine within a short space of time since I came off the plane from Canada.

He asked my cousins to buy two chickens, a bucket, clay pots and pieces of black material. When my cousins came back, we drove to the river. It was about an hour out of Kadoma. The place was filled with ritualistic paraphernalia. In the twilight, I made out red, white, green cloths, all tied up in fanciful ways, broken clay pots and other things I didn't know. We navigated down a narrow path to the edge of the water.

I wasn't looking forward to the cleansing. June is the winter season in Zimbabwe. It's freezing cold. I was already cold in the darkness and having icy water thrown on me wasn't the thing I had in mind. But, what could I do? When you're the Chosen. You have very little say in what happens to you.

"Oh," Musa turned to my cousins suddenly. "You forgot to buy the bucket."

"We didn't. We must've left it at your place," Wes was surprised. "Goodness, what do we do?"

"We use the clay pot," said me who wanted to get it over with. "It works just as good."

"No," Musa refused.

"Yes," I insisted. I wanted to go to my hotel room and sleep.

"No," he was firm. Turning to my cousins, he instructed, "you will have to go back."

"All the way back to town?" They replied at the same time. "That's a couple of hours there and back."

"It can't be helped. I need to do a good job."

"I still say we should use the clay pot." What the fuck was wrong with him? Wasn't he the one who went on and on about time and the lateness of the hour? Now he was going to make me sit by the side of this river for two hours!

I didn't like this plan. It seemed as if Musa organized for the bucket to be forgotten. I couldn't put it past him. After all, he desperately wanted me to spend a few days in his God forsaken town.

I however, had a more important issue to think about. I still couldn't see his ancestor. It was beginning to worry me. Did he have an ancestor at all? What if he had a Shavi? I stared deep into Musa's eyes, searching for the gleam. No bright, red diamond light. It meant nothing. I was still uneasy.

Musa literally harassed my cousins into going back to town. After they left, he took the first hour to teach me how to see metaphysical objects on top of water.

"Water is my element. My wife was worried about us coming to the river because the spirits come alive in the water at this time. Look into the horizon of the river and tell me what you see."

I peered in the direction he pointed at. "I see nothing."

"Don't use your eyes. Use your grandma."

I looked again and this time I saw a group of people dancing on water. They seemed to be following a man's directions. He enacted a step. They repeated it. There was quite a party going on.

"It's fuzzy, cos I'm short sighted," I told Musa. It took a few minutes before my mind opened. "I can see a group of people dancing. They're being led by a man."

"Describe them."

"They're dressed in dirty white." On closer reflection, they appeared to be one mass, rather than individuals. The man in front was the exception. When I first saw them, I thought they were dancing close to a bank because behind them was darkness. This time, however, I noticed, there was no bank. They were in the middle of the water. Where was the darkness coming from? Odd. "They're dancing on water."

"Follow the ripples of the water," he instructed.

Amazingly the ripples led to me.

"These are the souls of those who drowned and didn't make it into the continuum for one reason or another," my grandma said. "don't let the ripples lap your toes."

I stepped back. Musa noticed it.

"You know what they are?" he seemed more than interested.

"They're unclean."

"Very good. Why?"

I shrugged. "I don't know."

"Guess."

I didn't want to guess. I wanted my ritual and to high tail it out of there.

"Through no fault of their own, they died in servitude to the dark side. They probably didn't know they were harnessed. They went to witchdoctors and asked them to do dark spells on others, not knowing the witchdoctor could do the same to them because their requests earned them a one-way ticket to enslavement," Grandma explained.

"What kind of rituals would these people have wanted?"

"Wealth rituals. They want to harness someone. Most don't start there. They begin with the little things. They want a specific person to fall in love with them or they want revenge because a person they loved dumped them. They want a friend to lose her job, or an enemy to have hard times. Basically, they want to control another's life for their own gain. It leads to their ultimate destruction. The seven deadly sins in the white man's book aren't a lie."

Grandma was talking about:

1. Lust
2. Gluttony
3. Greed
4. Sloth
5. Wrath
6. Envy
7. Pride

"Look at the surface of the water again," Musa interrupted our internal conversation.

My eyes were now trained. All I had to do was let Grandma use my eyes and she picked up what I needed to see. I fully expected more sinful souls who had no idea they were harnessed while they were making other people's lives miserable.

What I saw instead, took my breath away. A Unicorn. I was transfixed. A beautiful, dainty, elegant shimmering blue light encased horse ran leisurely on the water's surface. It's horn, stuck on its forehead, gleamed gold while its wings, almost butterfly like, radiated with colors of the rainbow. The creature was pure light. I'd never seen anything so beautiful. I was transfixed.

A unicorn? In Africa of all places. Forget Africa. In the metaphysical! It crossed the water and disappeared into the horizon.

"Don't forget to look for physical evidence," Musa redirected my gaze.

Of course. The water. I looked down and there were the gentle ripples, making their way to our bank. It really wasn't in my head. I was thrilled beyond. Never, in my eyes as a disciple of the metaphysical had I seen anything so ethereal. Definite evidence of God's existence.

"You learn fast. Can we sit down and talk?"

It was obvious class was over. I found a nice little rock to perch my tired ass on. Musa stood in front of me and gave me a prediction.

"You're going to meet a man very soon."

I really wasn't interested in hearing about my romantic life. "I haven't had a boyfriend for almost ten years."

"You're going to have one. Soon."

I didn't reply. I always got told I was gonna meet a man. It never happened. Romance was one of the things blocked in my metaphysical. I worked on unblocking it for years, and miserably failed. At some point I gave it up and readjusted my thinking. Being without a partner or sex was okay. There were upsides to living alone.

If I lived with a man, I couldn't sleep with my dogs. Perhaps my son wouldn't be so free and happy. I couldn't stay in bed all day if I chose. I probably would've to cook more often. Moreover, I could work as much as I wanted without someone complaining I wasn't paying attention to them.

The most important thing was, I could wake up at three am to do my rituals. There were days when I was immersed in the metaphysical twenty-four seven. My son was used to it. A man would probably complain.

As a single woman, I was good.

"What's your status?" he suddenly asked. The man was an expert at interrupting my thoughts.

"Excuse me?" What status? What was he talking about?

"Your HIV status," he explained.

127

"Huh?" Shock wasn't the word. What did my status have to do with anything?

"Are you positive?" He took my hand to massage my wrist.

"I'm HIV negative," I informed him, wondering what kind of ritual required this information. He caressed my wrist some more, making me uncomfortable. Out of respect, I didn't pull away. The man was the doctor here, not me. He knew what he was doing. Hopefully.

"You have such clear veins. I can see the blue of your blood."

"Okay?" I waited for where this was going.

"You have a seductive personality. When witchdoctors see you, they forget their job. They want to sleep with you. Because you exude a great sexuality. You tempt them, like Delilah."

"Okay?" This was weird. But, whatever. I took my wrist back.

"Tempting men is a sin. It is a bad spirit to be sexy. You know it right?"

"No." Clearly, this guy was old school. Women were not supposed to be beautiful, nor sexy in the old days. Ugly and none descript were good.

"Someone put the spirit on you. It was a great disservice."

I didn't think so. And why was it his business?

He seemed to read my thoughts. "Witchdoctors don't really work on you with gusto because they want you. I, on the other hand, am not like them. I'm very professional. I see you."

"What do you see?" I was curious.

"The second I saw you, I wanted you. Then I realized, no, it's a bad spirit."

We were back to that again?

"You were about to tell me what you see in me." He needed to be led. I was there for the job.

"You're bleeding."

He was right. From every pore of my skin.

"You have been metaphysically suppressed, oppressed, abused and used."

Very good. I was loving the sympathy in his voice. I'd been wrong all along about this man. He was not only kind and sympathetic, he was also professional. I should like him. I resolved to do it. I would work hard on it. He didn't deserve my suspicions. He proved it with his next words.

"I'm going to help you. I'm going to help you beat your enemies. After I'm done with you, no one will ever invade your space to harm you again."

Chapter 7

The African American Soldier.

"Grandma, the one thing he gave me and not Wes or Greg was oil." I remembered just before I went to bed. "He told me it was for good travels. He said I should use it on my face, handbag and luggage."

"You found it! The oil opened the portal from his world to yours. We need to close it. Go to bed. I'll have a solution tomorrow morning."

Portals opened and closed in my world on a regular basis. They were usually from the veil. One of my jobs in this world is to walk the transcended to their final resting place. It is part of being a witchdoctor. I've walked Bantus to the Left mostly. I've only ever escorted two people to the Peak. They were both men. One was a drunk in his life and another lived with autism.

The Right collects its own people. We don't have an idea how they go about doing it.

No one surprised me more than an African American soldier who died in Africa on a secret mission. I was done with my dinner one evening when the portal opened and in he walked into my living room.

"What's going on?" he asked.

It's always sad when they don't know they've transcended because somehow, they've ended up at a place they had no idea of its existence. I imagined this young man of about twenty-four and still dressed in his military fatigues, had been a Baptist, as were most African Americans. He must have expected to go to the Baptist afterlife. Yet, here he was, standing in my living room. He was confused.

"You're with the Bantu," I informed him, already retrieving my grandfather's walking stick from the wall. I was gonna need it.

"The Bantu?"

"You've transcended and God sent you to us," I explained.

"What?"

"I mean you're dead!" Time to use language he understood. "You're here because this is your religion."

"I'm a Baptist." He was indignant.

"Clearly, God decided otherwise. He categorized you as one of us. You must have a lot of Bantu DNA." It was the only thing I could think of.

There may have been other reasons as to why he ended up with us. He died in West Africa, among the Nilotes. It was possible he could've gone into the Nilotic continuum and they booted him to us. Or, Christianity didn't want him. Sometimes religions rejected their own. He may also have chosen us and didn't remember. I'd walked many souls to the left who chose us. Perhaps there was an office of some kind where souls went. They were probably orientated on all the "countries" they could go to and chose us. Those souls always told me they'd been sent to me, since they had no idea how to go about being accepted into our continuum. I often called myself their immigration customs officer. My one question to them was always, "Why us?"

The answer was always the same, "you're the only ones who will have me."

There was a soul who said our compassion and forgiveness was what made him choose us. I remember feeling all mushy and special after he said it.

This young man's demeanor however, told me he didn't get any orientation. He most certainly didn't choose us. We were as much a surprise to him as he was to me.

"What is Bantu?"

"An African tribe," I explained. "Some of your ancestors must have come from us. They claimed you."

There were many occasions when Bantu ancestors claimed souls on account of their DNA. A lot of white Africans have Bantu DNA and have ended up in the continuum because their Bantu ancestors wouldn't let them go.

"It means I belong." He took the information in his stride.

"You have arrived son of the soil," I welcomed him.

"You say I'm dead?" He was in the non-believing mode. It happens to those who die suddenly.

"Can you see my face?"

"You're beautiful," they all compliment me when they transcend. I think they see me in another way and not my physical form.

"Thank you," I smiled. "Since you can see my face, you're dead."

"Fuck!" He threw out the expletive softly. He didn't have the energy to say it with more strength. He was exhausted. To the bone. Dying isn't easy.

"What happened?"

"I was fighting. I got shot I guess," he was resigned.

"No need to guess," I teased. There was no need to get morbid. Transcending was a beautiful thing. He'd left all the suffering of the human experience behind. This was a new chapter, full of light, hopefully. Besides, he had a very strong Bantu ancestor who was waiting for him. He would be protected and loved. He was never going to walk alone. "We can safely say you were shot."

"Yeah," he smiled for the first time. He was getting with the program.

"You'll be home soon. I envy you."

"You do?"

"Yes. You came, you saw, you did. Your journey is over."

He took a moment to digest what I said. Then he surprised me. "My wife. She's pregnant. We're having our second child."

When one transcended, the memories of their lives were supposed to be wiped out. When I transcended due to the machinations of my mother, I became the little girl again who lived in the village with Marita and Michael. God took me back to my happiest moment. I wasn't a mother who'd left behind a son. I didn't remember him.

I'd never met anyone who remembered their immediate past and the people they left behind. This soldier was unusual.

"God to keep her and your children safe in his right fist." I said softly.

It came to me then that his wife and children were his happiest place.

"Do you remember anyone else?" I asked, just to test my theory.

He took a moment to think it through. He frowned. "No. Should I?"

His wife and him were lucky to have found true love.

"No," I replied.

"Tell her I love her."

"I don't know her."

"She will be in the newspapers. Find her."

"I will try."

"What happens now?"

"Now I kneel and thump the floor three times with my grand-father's walking stick. I'll do a little chant. We wait five minutes and then you are home."

I held my grandfather's walking stick in both hands, hit the ground with one end three times and chanted. "Hail the realm of the ancestors. Your son is at your door. Please open for him."

I ululated before I stood up.

"That's it?" he wasn't impressed.

"Yeah."

"Now what?"

"We wait."

The reply was quick. It always is in these circumstances. It comes in the powerful redirection of my energy to where the person is supposed to go. I find myself turning to the Left, right or looking ahead with a force I can't put into words.

"Take three steps to the Left," I informed him.

"This is it?" He was asking if he had finally reached his destination.

"Yeah. Son of the soil, you're home."

"What's waiting for me?" He wasn't afraid. No one ever is. He was curious.

He knew nothing about where he'd ended up in the veil. I felt awful for him.

"Reincarnation, redemption and lots of hard work. Congratulations!" I meant it. I fully hoped to go to the Left after my human experience was done. I was too much of a sinner to make it to the Peak. Although I certainly had no intention of doing evil, I couldn't be sure one day I wouldn't succumb to it. Nevertheless, I was going to fight going to the Right side by always doing right by mine own.

He smiled. "I ain't afraid of hard work."

I smiled back, "neither am I."

The portal opened. Blue light bathed the entry way, instead of the circle of fire. I was taken aback. For as long as I've been escorting people to the Left, there's always been a ring of fire to collect them. They would get a scolding from the female voice coming from within and then they would be burned to ash before their ashes joined the ring of fire. My father went the same way.

The door of blue light, therefore, was something new for me. This American soldier was going first class! I was impressed. He'd done something right in his life.

"Son of the Soil. You have arrived," the female voice welcomed him joyously. "Time to rest."

He gave me one last whimsical look. "Is this good?"

He meant the blue lighted door.

I nodded. "Very good."

The American soldier needed a little more companionship. He hesitated and looked to me for more guidance.

"We're Bantu. We never walk alone," I wanted to be there for him. "Take three steps forward," I encouraged.

I took the steps with him. "I'm walking with you."

The African American soldier was my first and only experience of someone who went to the Left and got rest immediately. When I escorted my father, the woman wasn't impressed to see him.

"You're back again! You don't learn. I have a lot of hard work for you this time! You deserve it. I'm tired of you coming back. I had high hopes you would change."

Oddly, before the ring of fire burst in front of us, my dad, besides apologizing to me for stealing my ancestors and ruining my life, confessed he was tired. The human experience had been too difficult for him. His transition even more so because he died unexpectedly.

The next morning, I told Agnes about the African American soldier who died on a secret mission to Africa and ended up under the Bantu zip code.

"African Americans are Bantu too. They have our DNA! I could be walking lots of them to the Left in the future."

"It could be because he died in West Africa," Agnes pointed out. "I mean, a lot of our colonizers ended up in our continuum hence the white ancestors. We also have Indian ancestors. They came to Africa and died there too. I don't think all African Americans are going to die in Africa. You won't have lots of them coming your way."

"No. It wasn't because of where he died. Grandma told me he was part Bantu. His soul found its way home, albeit not the home he expected. Grandma said he was sent to me so he wouldn't walk alone."

"Oh," Agnes had to think about it. "I never saw them as part of us. They identify more with West Africans, even though the first slaves to land in New York were Bantu."

Learning from Agnes, who's country had lots of people shipped into slavery by the Portuguese was an eye opener.

"There's no doubt there are many African Americans with Bantu DNA," I reasoned.

"I guess," Agnes acquiesced. "It's just hard to believe because they only recognize West Africans."

"Perhaps they don't know."

"They soon will, with DNA testing."

My girl is more Bantu in thought and deed than I am. I tend to embrace and learn from differences. She is a stickler. There was a time we wrote a spell for the type of men we wanted. She was specific. He had to be Bantu, from Southern Africa. Nothing else would do. For me, it didn't matter.

"Anyway, get this," I changed the subject, "He told me I was going to see his wife in the newspapers. He asked me to reach out to her, tell her he loves her. That's impossible."

He wasn't wrong. They never are when they transcend. It took a few days for the story of an African American soldier who died in West Africa under mysterious circumstances to hit the press. He'd somehow been separated from his unit. It took days for his body to be found. I recognized his face from the images on CNN. It ran with his story relentlessly. There were questions, government statements, even from Trump. I was astounded.

Furthermore, his funeral was televised. His wife and family wore white to his funeral. I was taken by the woman he loved so much. She represented him well, with her quiet dignity and beauty. She chose to wear white. For some Bantu tribes, it is the color of death. I knew she wore it for another reason, yet, it was still such a wonderful tribute to a man who went into the Bantu continuum in style.

Although he didn't make it to the peak, he was still right up there with those who did good.

I still haven't given his wife the message because I don't know her. It's not easy looking for people and giving them messages from the dead. Most don't take it kindly.

More importantly for me, I decided to break the code of secrecy and share my religion and spirituality with everyone. This thing of the Bantu, it belonged to the world because the Bantu are in the world.

Unfortunately for me, Musa's portal had nothing to do with the celestial doorways. It came from the North. A blatant attack on my person.

Chapter 8

Day 3

2:45 am

The Capture

"Wake up," Grandma's voice slid into my mind at two forty-five am the next day. It took me a good fifteen minutes to gain any sort of cognisance. "Today, we're going to show Musa some things."

Grandma sounded ominous. I liked it. On my way to the basement, grandma asked me to grab four lemons.

"Mix some tobacco with water. Program it. Then draw a large triangle behind you with the Peak facing your altar using the water and tobacco solution."

This was something new. I was learning in leaps and bounds.

"How do I program the tobacco?"

"Kneel, grab it in your hand and raise the fist high. Say, "let nothing that steps into the triangle leave. It will belong to us, to do with as we wish.""

It took very little time after I drew the triangle and once again took my position at the altar, back turned to my artistry before Musa's slave had something to say. He brought with him, as usual, a very cold chill. It was a good thing I was prepared, wrapped in my cloak as I was.

"You're extremely annoying"! He was bothered I hadn't followed instructions.

"Ignore him," grandma advised. "Instead, look to your North. We have uncovered the portal. He is watching us."

I turned slightly to my north and there Musa was, staring at me, taking note of everything going on. The portal was the size of a mid-sized wall mirror. I could see he was sitting in a room with an old brown closet. The room was as dark as he was, except his eyes. There it was, the bright, diamond spark. It wasn't red like my mother's or any of the other dark practitioners I was familiar with. This one was a feverish brownish blue. Interesting.

"The dark spirit found a way of hiding it's true nature," grandma explained the difference in colors. "Like your father."

"Musa is a high-level dark spirit?" My dad was a high-level dark practitioner.

They functioned differently from the lower level dark practitioners like my mother. They were more discerning, coldly ruthless rather than passionately and strove to make subtle, yet effective changes to the world.

My dad never killed anyone using the metaphysical world, unlike my mother. At the last count, twenty-three people had died in my family because of my mother and her coven. Killing was beneath my dad.

He often said there were worse things than death. He dealt in them. He destroyed dreams, set up chain reactions of misery and enslaved hundreds of people. I was one of his slaves.

I broke free by myself. It was an enlightening moment because at the time, I had no idea my father was a dark skills practitioner. I was still in the dark about my role and purpose as well. It started as a waking dream. In the dream I was imprisoned in a clay pot kept under my bed at our holiday home. The clay pot was covered with a piece of material. I was desperate to get out. Using my hands, I banged against the cloth. It took hours before the binding around the cloth gave and I pulled myself out of the pot.

As I stumbled out, gasping, I noticed my cousin Wes and my sister Rumbi were also in this pot. Behind them, were lots of other people too.

"Wes," I called him, "we're free! Get out quickly. We've got to run."

My cousin struggled out of the pot, followed by my sister. My sister's appearance shocked me. She looked like a three-year old, instead of the twenty-nine-year-old she was in real life. I looked at myself and realized I was about twelve years old. What the hell?

"We've got to go!" I was frantic.

I led the way out of our house. We all scattered about the yard, some of us crawling onto the roof, including Wes and Rumbi. I, on the other hand was driven to the center of the lawn. There was something I had to dig out of the earth. It was situated right there. I went for it, scrapping the grass and soil with my fingers. I dug, frightened I would be caught.

My dad appeared out of nowhere. In his hand was a wooden stick which resembled a walking stick, but not quite. The design purported it to be something else. Since I'd never seen such a thing in my life, I didn't know what it was.

He was livid. Ignoring all the other people, he came straight for me.

"You have been a problem to me since the day you were born!" My usually contained father raged. "I will kill you!"

He was about to strike me with the stick when something lifted me off the ground and flew me into the sky. From my aerial view I could see my sister, Wes and various other people still on the roof.

What was that? I was shell shocked. It took me a moment to realize I wasn't asleep, nor had I been dreaming. What the hell happened?

I called my dad. After I finished sharing the experience with him, he said, "so now you know."

"What do I know?" I was dazed.

"I kept you in chains since you were twelve years old. You broke free. Does it hurt?"

"Dad," was all I could say. I was drained of energy.

This urban, highly educated, handsome, charming and successful man was the love of my life. Moreover, he didn't believe in spirituality. He spent his entire life telling us believing in a higher power and metaphysical stuff was for those who couldn't deal with their true selves.

"Human beings," he always said, "are inherently cruel. Its who we are. We make up gods and goodness to stop ourselves from doing the unspeakable. We think it's unspeakable, but it's not. It is natural and the way of things. We use spirituality to fight against our true natures."

"Does what hurt?" I finally blubbered.

"I stunted your growth. You may be twenty-seven physically, but you're actually twelve years old. You were difficult to harness. I locked you up the day you were born, but you kept escaping. I finally succeeded when you were twelve. I'm disappointed you escaped again, but at least my binding held for fifteen years. Not bad. I need to tweak it a little more."

"Dad?" I whimpered.

What was the love of my life saying? He was the only person I had. My dad was extremely loving towards me. He freed me from aunt Juliet's house when I cried one day about living there. He immediately put a stop to it, no questions asked. He was the one who picked me up at school when I was ill. He drove me to out of town to cheerleading meets, secretly gave me pocket money, a credit card to boot. He stopped my mother from beating me. At one point he pulled her off me and threw her against the wall.

Furthermore, he was the one I ran to when life didn't go my way. He was my safety zone, the place where all things were possible. Dad was the only person I had. I loved him more than life itself.

"Does this hurt you?" he was cold. "If it does, find your God. I'm sure you'll find solace in him."

He cut the phone, making it the last conversation we had until the day he died many years later.

I was left knowing I hadn't been dreaming. The betrayal was hard.

How could Musa, gross and dirty, be like my dad? The person I was staring at through his portal was unable to reign in his emotions. He was excited, overly so in anticipation for what he thought was gonna go down. He was just too emotional, obsessed and in my opinion too crazy to be anything like my dad.

"Be careful about calling evil people crazy," grandma warned, as she'd done many times. "Crazy is a catch all phrase the white man created. Crazy doesn't exist. When a person exhibits who they are, we're quick to label them so we can be comfortable. Musa is most certainly not at the same level as your dad. Your dad, my son, was the apex of dark practitioners, as you are at the apex of Light practitioners. Musa is mid-level. Your mother is the bottom of the barrel."

I closed my eyes to dispel the memories of my dad. It didn't matter what he did to me. I still loved him above everyone else.

"Thank you for continuing to love him." Grandma's tone was gentle. "This is what makes you exceptional."

"He threw me a birthday party," I whispered to grandma. "With caterers, tents and everything. Everyone came. When I saw the preparations, I put my hand in his, looked up at him and asked, "daddy, what is this for?"

"He said it was for your birthday because you were a very special little girl who should be celebrated," grandma finished.

"Yeah," I wiped the tears. "Every year on my birthday...."

I couldn't finish. Grandma did. "He sent you a large bouquet of flowers, something he didn't do for his other children. You were and are special. He couldn't help but acknowledge it."

A river of tears. I didn't want to be special. I wanted to be loved by those I gave love to. What an unattainable goal for me. It broke my heart.

"I said Musa's watching us," grandma redirected me, as she always did when my heart was involved.

I came back to reality fast. I focused. There was a war to be won.

"Did he see us draw the triangle?"

"No, he came with his spirit. This spirit is capable of walking past his defences. When it walked the earth as human, it was Chosen."

"Hence the ability to break through any defences." I mused. "Did Musa kill him?"

"Yes. He spent years devoting himself to his ancestors in a bid for wealth. As a small business owner, he believed his ancestors' job was to make him rich. He didn't realize there was no wealth given to ancestors by God. The wealth is given to the soul. God hadn't given him great wealth. When he discovered the truth, he went to Musa. He wanted to be rich."

I knew what happened after. "Musa harnessed the relatives of the man who had metaphysical wealth. For a while there, this man was a slave owner."

"Yes," grandma agreed. "Unfortunately, Musa harnessed and then killed him. He took as much money in payment from this young man before he bagged him."

"Why kill him?"

"For many reasons. Harnessed metaphysical wealth doesn't last in the hands of the thief. A lot of slaves were therefore needed to maintain the wealth. It wouldn't have worked in the long run. Musa knew it. To protect his reputation, the man had to go. Witchdoctors are only as good as their reputation. If Musa couldn't keep this man rich, the man was going to damage him. Moreover, this man had metaphysical powers. He may not have appreciated them, but they were worthy of harvesting. Musa is using them now."

"Why kill him though?" I asked again.

"Powers are weak without the energy God designated them to. In the end child, they will kill you."

I knew this and it hurt my heart to no end. They weren't going to succeed. I deserved to die in God's time. I'd earned it by not killing myself when I wanted to.

"You surprise us," Grandma addressed the spirit of the man who died in his mid-thirties.

The spirit brimmed with fury behind me. His energy was disjointed, darker than the last time too. I felt it without having to look. "What surprises you?"

It came out as more of a sneer than anything else. I could feel his energy boring into my back, desperate to reach me. He wanted to possess me and was actively working on it. Had I been facing him, he might've enveloped my energy, swallowed me whole in fact.

154

Musa's expression suddenly made sense to me. This spirit was here to hunt. And I was the prey.

"You're serving the man who killed you."

"He didn't," the spirit objected.

"You don't remember," grandma was all sympathy. "Of course. He made sure of it. Where do you think you are?"

"I'm waiting to join the continuum. Musa is walking with me."

"In the meantime, you help out a friend?"

"Yes."

"Wrong."

"What does this have to do with anything? You were asked to remove all of Musa's herbs from your house since you no longer wanted to work with him. We said we would leave!" The spirit was angrily impatient with grandma.

"He will leave," grandma screamed in rage.

I lost my balance on the mat from the force of it and nearly fell into the candles. I felt my grandma pull her energy back fiercely for my protection. I shuffled a little more to the right when I gained my balance. It was wise to move away when elephants fought.

"He will leave," grandma repeated. "Whether he likes it or not. You, on the other hand, are not going anywhere."

Say what now?

"Grab the clay pot," grandma urged.

"We don't have a clay pot. I left them in Zimbabwe with Tete Retina."

"No matter. Get a jar. Make sure it has a lid."

The cold of my basement turned to heat. I realized it was coming from the spirit. I caught the sight of Musa as I went up the stairs to my kitchen where I had jars, for playing the do it yourself woman when it came to pickling things. He was frantically chanting.

"He's trying to retrieve his friend," grandma explained. "He knows what we're about to do."

"What are we doing?" I was excited.

Grandma addressed the spirit. "We see you don't mind being imprisoned. That's good, because we're changing your prison. We will become your wardens before we hand you to the Right. They're missing their citizen."

"There's nothing you can do to me," he hissed arrogantly. Dark spirits, like dark people are very arrogant and disrespectful in general. "You're just whores, filthy and weak! If you had any power at all, Musa wouldn't have been able to get close."

"We will see."

Grandma stopped me before I sat on the mat with my jar.

"Face him."

I'd never in my life looked directly at an energy unrelated to me. What greeted me was a blackness I'd never seen. It was dense, with darker little particles circulating around it. The energy was also tall. From my basement floor to the ceiling. Furthermore, it vibrated to the extreme.

I looked at my hopeless little green jar and back at it in doubt.

"He will fit," grandma asserted.

The energy laughed in contempt. "I can't be imprisoned by the likes of you! You're females! You're seducers, adulterers, garbage! You shouldn't ever have seen the light of day. This god of yours, how is he godly when brings back an uncultured, sinful being who broke every code of her people? You belong to us. You should be helping instead of fighting us."

No doubt, he was talking about my grandma.

"I was a sinner to the people. Not to God," grandma countered. "For my sin to the living, I'm paying my debt. You, on the other hand haven't begun to pay. But you will."

"What sort of ancestors choose a conduit such as this one?" he raged.

It was my turn to be insulted.

"She's lost her culture, resides among foreigners and bore a foreigner a child. She's filthier than you."

Ouch!

"Noted." Grandma wasn't about to trade insults. "Let's get to work. Kneel between the peak outside the triangle."

The spirit tried to break free of the triangle. He hit every angle, coming close enough for me to back off at the peak.

"Don't worry. Our confines are keeping his energy in check. This is the power of tobacco, water and all of us."

She was right. As much as the spirit tried to come at me, his energy remained imprisoned.

"Kneel!"

These were the surreal times! It was a dazed me who made sure the angle of the peak was between my knees.

"Open the jar! Extend it above your head."

I'd barely lifted the jar before grandma ordered me to hail the ancestors.

A direct possession happened immediately. A mighty force, greater than one I'd ever felt, slid into my body. A new language and voice made its way out of my mouth. All I knew was there was a man who was in my body, talking through me. The language was familiar. I'd heard it before, a million times. That was about it.

"Put the jar down and pick up your grandfather's walking stick." I heard my grandma's voice from a distance. I was floating inside of myself, light-headed and strangely happy. The force within brought a lot of love, protection and comfort to me. It said, "move away from this mess my child. I've got this." I'd never felt this cherished in my entire life.

I grasped the walking stick. It wasn't an easy task because my brain wasn't connecting with my body as it should.

"Stand up and thrust the stick into the energy."

I remember passion, heat, righteousness being the emotions flowing through me. The voice verbalized stronger. It reverberated throughout my basement. What basement? I personally was somewhere else, perhaps in the veil. I didn't know. My energy was a distant spectator in this ritual.

I was somewhere safe, floating in the clouds, in great peace.

I found myself abruptly back on my knees, granddad's walking stick in the jar. A loud howl escaped from the spirit which moments ago proudly spouted insults and Musa's loathing of me blasted from the portal at the same time. Grandma held it back with the flick of her hand. It was overwhelming. Thank God grandfather was there.

I watched the energy follow the walking stick into the jar as if from a long way away. The thing fit.

"Close the jar!"

I did and suddenly fully came to. Grandfather had disengaged. What an experience!

"Put your hand over the jar. Say, "What we've sealed, can never be broken by anyone except us."

After I was done, I placed the jar at my altar, behind the candles.

"Look to the North wall. Musa is losing it," grandma was triumphant.

Indeed, he was. He was counter chanting, angrily trying to open the jar. I stared at the jar in awe. A man's soul was in there. How small we human beings were in this great universe. We were less than chicken.

"Take the lemons we brought. Chant over them."

"Hail the lemon which came from the earth and was nurtured by water, wind and the sky, please do your purpose. Close the portal and cut all communications between myself, Musa and every other soul who has linked themselves to me against my will for eternity."

I'd barely finished the chant before Musa's portal closed with a loud bang. I practically saw three metaphysical walls go up. The first was red, the second white and the last black. Wow, a chant on a bunch of lemons were responsible? The metaphysical world never ceased to amaze me. The smallest of God's creations made the biggest difference.

"Squeeze the lemons. Pour them in bathwater. Use the rest of them to scrub yourself from head to toe."

"Yes, grandma."

"He will never be able to open the portal again in your direction." Grandma was satisfied. "We will ask for instructions tomorrow morning on how to deposit this soul into the proper hands. We don't keep darkness with us longer than we have to."

"We're done for today?" I was hopeful.

"Yes."

I was about to rise off the mat when a clear voice announced itself.

"Ntombizodwa." The name encompassed the entire basement.

Chapter 9

Grandma Shopedzai

W hat. Was. That? Oh, dear God! I couldn't catch a break. I was probably gonna need two jars. I didn't think I had another. Too bad for me.

Grandma and I went still. Oddly, there was no change of atmosphere. Everything remained calm, as if something ethereal hadn't announced its name. I figured if we waited long enough, the name dropper would go away. I counted the seconds, breathed out in relief because nothing else happened and proceeded to rise.

"Ntombidzodwa."

Leaving was out of the question. Back on my knees, facing away from the voice.

Who the heck was Ntombizodwa? This wasn't a Shona name. It was more like Zulu or Xhosa. I was going to google it when I was done with the court. I could feel my whole back rising in anticipation. Weird. I wasn't scared. This energy held a familiarity I couldn't put my finger on it. It wasn't here to harm me. I was sure of it, for a second, before I changed my mind.

"Ntombizodwa," the spirit introduced itself for the third time, this time closer to my right side.

"Grandma?" the uncertainty came through. Fear won the day.

"Remain where you are," Grandma wasn't feeling any trepidation. "Let's see what she will do."

"She?"

"She said she was Ntombizodwa. It's a girl's name." My grandma's tone was like, "are you stupid or what?"

I literally giggled.

"She's introduced herself three times. We will know whether she's friend or foe soon."

Numbers are important in the metaphysical. There are spells which have to be chanted on once, three, or seven times. Courts are given number designations too, depending on the reason. To ask for favor, for instance, one opened the court on three consecutive mornings before a reply is given. To wage a war, as I was doing, I had to go for two straight weeks before knowing whether we'd won or not. Repelling an illness took five or ten courts. There's a science to this shit.

Foes only introduce themselves once. As in the spirit we imprisoned. They also don't give a name. This was a new experience to me. My ancestors came to me nameless. It took two years for Grandma to tell me her name. She didn't do it to me. She did it to her daughter, my Tete Retina.

I was on the phone with my aunt, organizing the transcension I'd just been through. My aunt was being uncooperative, not wanting anything to do with it.

"I'm a woman," she said. "Talk to your fathers about this."

She knew there was no love lost between my fathers, i.e, my dad's younger brothers and myself. For many years I turned to them for help. They gave me none.

Grandma decided to put an end to the stalemate. She took over my body, a very rare occurrence, and spoke to her daughter herself.

"Retina, this is your mother, Shopedzai."

My aunt gasped in horror or whatever. I couldn't be sure, because you know, I had no idea I was with grandma Shopedzai.

Grandma Shopedzai was a hated character by the entire clan. Grandma, a product of undeniable love between her parents was born from scandal. Her mother, my great grandmother, fell in love with her husband's younger brother. She was in her late thirties and said brother, early twenties.

When my great grandmother married, she became mom to her husband's much younger brothers, for their mother was dead. The little boys lived with her and the babies she dropped into the household. They were age mates, more like brothers and sisters than uncles, nieces and nephews.

My grandma's dad, the oldest of the brood, was sent to work in the goldmines in South Africa when he was little more than twelve. He didn't return for a visit until his twenty first year.

My great grandmother and great grandfather looked at each other and fell hard. It took no time for them to hit the mat, as we say in Zimbabwe. Clearly, the mother/son bond was history. My great grandfather took to coming home often. He stayed longer and longer, to the whole village's happiness for he was not only modern, he lived in South Africa. It made him exotic. He was also very good with his hands. He repaired people's rickety gadgets, spend money on seeds for the clan and helped build huts.

In the process, he built himself a house, a proper house, the way a white man would. It was clear he wasn't going to reside in the house permanently. My great grandfather was still residing and working in South Africa. He came when he could.

No one thought anything of it when my great grandmother packed her shit and moved into the newly built house, along with her husband and children.

"She raised him," they said. "She is his mother. It is only fitting and right he should take care of her."

A few months later however, it became the talk of the entire village when my great grandfather returned and threw out everyone, except my great grandmother.

"What the fuck?" they said.

They were still saying it when my great grandmother became pregnant and gave birth to my grandmother.

Never in the history of the village had someone openly stolen his brother's wife. A much older woman to boot. There were no more babies in their union. My grandmother's siblings were all from her mother's first husband.

To add insult to injury this child of a scandalous union, she was beautiful. The people felt there was no justice in the world. At sixteen, she found herself pregnant. She refused to name the daddy. She was later to tell me before she fell in love and got pregnant, she'd been sexually abused multiple times by uncles, cousins and even her brothers because of her beauty.

Anyway, my great grandfather, not wanting his daughter to suffer any more societal ills as a single mother, arranged a marriage for her with the local chief, the man I knew as my grandfather, Zachariah. He was forty-two and a widower with three daughters. His daughters were older than my grandma.

Grandma objected. She preferred single motherhood. No one gave a damn. She entered a rocky marriage against her will. My dad was born a year after she gave birth to my aunt Ada. Rumor had it he wasn't my grandfather's son. The rumors were stamped down with a mighty force and life carried on.

My grandma's life plans didn't have an old husband and children in mind. She left my grandfather for another man and village within two years. She bore him two children, whom she brought back to the village when she left the dude. She was to repeat this cycle five more times.

Eventually, she gave up on men, settled back in her father's house and began to rebuild her life, using her hands. She was a master farmer, bringing in enviable harvests every year. She was also a terrible mother. Shopedzai had no interest in her children. She told me motherhood wasn't her thing. Had she been born in a different culture she would never have had children. Well, she lived her truth. She barely knew her children. In fact, she forgot some of them.

My dad remembered meeting her at a shopping center when he was in his teens. This is how it went down.

Grandma approached my dad and conversationally said, "you look familiar. Do I know you?"

My dad knew his mom. It hurt him to the core. He went to his grave with this story.

"You're my mother," he said.

"Oh, my goodness, yes!" She laughed. "You're my second born. No wonder you look familiar. What's your name?"

My dad's heart bled. "Elisha."

"Of course," she trilled delightedly. "Well, hello."

This encounter might be nothing to most people until you learn my grandmother lived only fifteen kilometers away from my granddad and her children.

To add insult to injury, my grandma was wealthy, on village terms, while my granddad, who was now very old, was poor. Chiefs were taken care of by the village through food, not cash. My dad started working at seven years of age and put himself through school, while my grandma, with her skill for farming wasn't short of coin. She sold her produce at the market in the capital city called Salisbury in her time. The villagers wouldn't touch it.

They abhorred and ostracized her. She'd broken every rule made by God and society when it came to women. She behaved like a man and they wouldn't have it. To top it all off, she was still beautiful.

On the call with my aunt, she apologized. "I wasn't a good mother. I was sent back, earlier than most to atone for my sins. I can't rest in the continuum because of who I was. I am sorry I caused you a lot of pain in your human experience. You met a bad mother and paid the price. I'm paying now. I want to rest like the others, and then walk into my reincarnation. I can't. I'm here, with my grandbaby, trying to save her from my own children. It doesn't surprise me her father embraced the dark side. I was a whore. Whores give birth to children who bow to the dark. It also doesn't shake me that he went after his own daughter. Nor am I shocked you all helped him. It's my fault. I'm undoing my own mess. Forgive me. Help your niece."

My aunt burst into tears. "You're my mother. You never have to apologize to me. I'm the one who should ask for forgiveness. As the child. I bow to you, not the other way around."

"We're waiting for her to say it again," grandma brought me back from the memories. "If she says it again, she belongs to us."

Oh, the suspense!

"Ntombizodwa." The voice was firm, resolute and right next to me. She'd stepped on the mat. The energy took form. I found myself staring into a woman about three hundred pounds large, with big breasts, hips and thighs. She had a tiny waistline. It demarcated her voluptuous shape into a bountiful top and bottom half. She was wearing a headdress of white beads. The beads caressed her shoulders and covered her forehead.

I blinked at the alien-ness of it all. This wasn't my culture. She was lost. I was positive. She turned to look at me and I saw my own face. It was older, chubbier, mine all the same. I was mesmerized. She sat next to me.

Chapter 10

Gogo Ntombizodwa

I'd always known I had two female ancestors. Except in my dreams, I'd never met the other one. In my dreams, I never saw her face. She came to me dressed in what I vaguely knew as Sangoma regalia. Sangomas are Zulu witchdoctors. Their cultural uniforms are more elaborate than Shona witchdoctors.' They wear all their ancestral colors at once and have astonishing head gears made of beads. Their necklaces are thick, covering almost their entire chests.

The Shona on the other hand, wear their colors for a purpose. Blue is my dominant color. It represents healing, clairvoyance and femininity. I hardly ever pull out my male ancestors' black and white cloaks. I use them during seances and when I am ill, for they protect me in the physical.

My necklaces also, are just strings, whereas the Sangomas have elaborate ones covering their chests. Sangomas paint their faces, unlike us. Ntombizodwa had no face paint and her primary colors were turquoise, black and white. Mostly white.

She wasn't Zulu nor was she a Sangoma. She was Xhosa, an Igqirhakazi, which means female healer. Grandma told me all this while I gazed at her in wonder. The first thing she did was completely get rid of the dark energy Musa sent my way when he was angry. My grandma had only held it at bay. Gogo Ntombizodwa cleared it.

"Child, say hello to Gogo Ntombizodwa," grandma prompted.

I was too dazed to say anything. The woman had my face.

"She was with us all along," grandma explained. "This war has made her manifest. We need her."

Still gaping. Eyes staring hard at this new energy.

"She doesn't want to be called grandma. You're to use the traditional name for grandma. Gogo."

Nothing from me. Not even a peep. I was in my own zone. The woman had my face!

"Gogo Ntombizodwa is your grandfather's mother."

That explained the face.

"You're lucky. You have your father's mother and your grandfather's mother. Gogo Ntombizodwa has got the gift of herbs. She's going to teach you how to listen to and use them."

Blink, blink.

"Today we buy herbs to create defensive and protective concoctions." grandma continued her one-sided conversation.

"Will she talk to me, like you do?" My first question. I was coming to.

"No. I am the only one who talks to you, no matter what. They say things through me. If you hear another voice in your head, know you've been bewitched."

She'd told me before. Pity, when it happened, I'd forgotten. A male voice spoke to me instead of her for weeks. I assumed it was one of my male ancestors and she was taking a break. I even presumed it was the Story Teller because I'd never heard his voice. The Story Teller spoke to me through feeling and images in my head.

I wasn't uncomfortable with this foreign entity, talking to it, taking advice and obeying.

His requests became weirder and weirder with time. They made me uncomfortable. Our little thing began to fall apart. Friction became the order of the day eventually. I missed my grandma and wanted her back. My desire for her was strong, it gave her more strength to push the spirit aside and take back her position.

The big million-dollar questions then were, who was this motherfucker and how had he managed to enter my core space? It turned out he belonged to Molly.

His uncovering was long and hard. I fell ill out of the blue one day in mid-September. I couldn't get out of bed. The illness dragged on. My doctor thought it was all in my head, as always. He asked me if I wanted anti-depressants. I refused them and went back to my misery. I would have to conquer this shit by myself.

By October, I finally decided to confide in Molly and asked for help. Her ancestors pulled me from the jaws of Nyanzira in the nick of time after all. I thought Nyanzira was up to his usual tricks when it came to my life. Of every witchdoctor who tried to kill me, Nyanzira came the closest to achieving the feat. He had the time, for one. He'd been working on me for close to twenty years. He had the blood connections. My mother, my aunts, cousins, sisters and Taurai. He also had the determination, for my male ancestors are supposedly one of a kind.

Completely believing Nyanzira was responsible for laying me out for more than a month, I trusted Molly. I did every ritual she told me to, without question, with two results. My health deteriorated to the point where I was soiling myself and a male voice took over from grandma.

"You've been working with this woman for months now, yet, you're at death's door," a voice whispered in my bedroom one evening. "Something's wrong."

I can only say this came from a good spirit, for, sometimes they mind your business. What can they do with themselves when they spend eons floating about, checking on the world for God? It is my uneducated opinion these souls were good, kind people who died without progeny. No nieces, nephews or anyone at all related to them by blood. They therefore avail themselves to those in need.

I wasn't trying to hear what the spirit said. Molly was the lead officiant at my first transcension. After transcension, my grandma's voice became clear in my head. Grandma brought good things into my life. It couldn't be her.

There was nothing I wouldn't do for Molly. I gave her the shirt off my back many times. I wanted to help her be the great witchdoctor. People needed to know how powerful and beautiful this woman was. The world had to meet her. To that end, I desperately tried to bring her to Toronto for a psychic fair. I was also toying with the idea of starting spiritual vacations with her in mind. Molly was my friend. My ride or die in the metaphysical. I adored her.

"Exactly!" the nosey spirit interjected. "Your friend. Think about it."

Very few people cared for me, I wailed internally. You want to take away one who does. No.

"Why don't you call her? Say to her, "why am I ill after I've gone through a transcension? Grandma says something went wrong with the ascension. Grandma says I was supposed to have the ritual done at another location, a secure one. With very few people, not hundreds."

No. It wasn't Molly. She brought me to my ancestors when the whole world blocked me. She deserved my loyalty.

"Prove me wrong," the persistent one continued. "Do it."

Knowing the spirit wouldn't leave unless I did it, I called Molly and left a voicemail.

She replied, the next day, hurling abuse at me. "You show off! You're so white with all that "let me help you shit." You're ignorant about your own culture and purpose. How dare you question my methods? Do you know me? Do as you're told and be grateful! For someone who's a free meal for everyone, you have some nerve questioning my methods! First, do something for yourself before you think you're superior. It doesn't matter what your ancestors can do. You're weak and stupid. Apologize or else! Let me tell you, the people who've made me angry have had some terrible things happen to them. I don't play. Make it a good apology."

The woman who made a living as a thief until she met and married her police officer husband came out with a vengeance. I was gutted. I'd been expecting something compassionate and helpful from her. I saw her, in my mind, giving me stronger spells and

178

helping me dispel the dark energy consuming me. Instead, she threatened me.

Why? What had I done to her to deserve this? The question gored at my guts relentlessly. She's my friend, my soul wailed. We talked about men, our dreams, hopes and motherhood. I bonded with her. She was also a female witchdoctor in a world dominated by men. I believed she was on my side. To the end.

"Reply in gratitude," the goody two shoes spirit, who'd proved herself right was still with me! I hadn't realized. What a bummer. "Say you're extremely grateful for everything she's done for you. Shower her with praise. Do not apologize. Understand this is the last conversation you will ever have with her."

I complied.

"Now, get rid of everything from the transcension. She touched and chanted on it before you. She gave it instructions. The instructions are coming to pass. You're living in them. Take everything to the river. Tell the materials, the walking sticks, the snuff, the knobkerrie, everything, that you're returning them back to their mother. When you get back, mop your house with lemon juice."

I can't. I'm too weak to move.

"Start moving! You will get stronger as you cleanse the dirt out of your life."

She was right. Early the next morning, grandma woke me up. She'd overpowered the evil spirit Molly replaced her with in my life.

I learned a truth from the experience. One's ancestors are only as strong as the person they're with.

I spent the afternoon with Agnes, buying herbs in Toronto. I'd first gone on the internet and looked for hoodoo and wicca websites. I read them as much as I could, making notes on the herbs they said protected and repelled bad spirits. There was no way I was going to order herbs from Zimbabwe. For one thing, they would take too long, and for another, I no longer trusted mine own, no matter who they were.

"Grandma says I have to adjust, move with the times, embrace my country and learn everything there is to know, from this world's perspective." To dispel a sudden itchy sensation I scratched my wrists frantically.

Agnes was doubtful. "They tell us African herbs are stronger my sister."

"We'll soon find out." I believed the same as her, but desperate times call for desperate measures, do they not? The itch wouldn't stop. My wrists were turning red from the abuse. What was this? I'd worn my bangles for years and never had an allergic reaction to them before.

"Are you even gonna know how to use them?" My bestie mirrored my thoughts.

"Grandma said the new gogo is going to help me."

"You can do it. You're stronger now. I'm still impressed you caught onto Musa this quickly. If I were you, I wouldn't trust any witchdoctor. You should suspect them all."

It ached to admit she was right. Grandma said the same thing.

"As much as you like Gushungo and the old grandmother from the village, don't talk to them again. We're gonna find they were up to no good in time," she mused. "It seems our own have gone bad. Some of them might do good things, occasionally. They saw you coming. They felt you were an easy target. You've lived out of the country for a very long time. You were also raised in the suburbs. It gives you the definite aura of someone far removed from the culture. When they look at you, they see a white person. You're a foreigner to them. In every way. They fall to the temptation of taking from you. They can't help it."

"Yeah." I was preoccupied with my itchy wrists. They were developing bumps. The wise thing to do was to remove my bracelets.

"What are you doing?" Agnes was alarmed. "Your bracelets keep you safe. Without them people will astral project you and shit."

"I know," I moaned. "For some reason, they've been giving me trouble since I came back from Zim. I don't think I need them now though. Taking them off isn't bad. I think I'm stronger now."

"Yeah," Agnes agreed in relief. "You probably don't need them."

I slid my bangles into my bag, feeling unencumbered.

Chapter 11

Talking Herbs

A burning pain in my chest, along with the inability to breathe woke me up. At first, I couldn't move. I lay paralyzed, a victim of excruciatingly hot pins and needles delving in and out of my rib cage. My heart felt like someone was squeezing it from the inside. I swear, I saw blood oozing from between the fingers of the perpetrator. I saw it drain into my body and poison the rest of my parts.

"Musa sent us a weapon. It found its target," grandma informed me. "Get up. Get your grandfather's cloak and wrap yourself in it."

I can't.

"You can and will. If you lay there for five more minutes, you will die."

I'm not afraid of death. In fact, I welcome it. I'm weary.

"Good. But not tonight. Do as you're told."

I embraced the pain as I dropped myself off the bed and on the floor. To cover the space between my bed and the shelf where I kept my ancestral materials, I crawled. Unwrapping my black and white cloak took more time than my grandma wanted. Finally, with relief, I was under the black and white.

I lay for a few seconds, in the same state as I was in bed. It took a few more for me to be able to breathe. The pain persisted. By now, we'd become close relatives. Physical pain is something I know in great detail. Fighting it only makes it worse. Go with it. Let it consume you.

"Take some tobacco. Boil it in water."

Oh, my goodness! How was I supposed to get to my kitchen?

"On all fours." Grandma had no mercy.

About fifteen minutes later, my head was buried under the black and white and I was breathing hot steam from the tobacco and water concoction. The pot where I'd boiled the water was also redecorating my room. It burned through the carpet where I'd placed it. There was no end to this nightmare.

Grandma urged me afterwards to get back into bed. The three am court was suspended until the next day.

"Only in sleep do we heal," she soothed. "We've managed to move Musa's weapon from you to mid-air. He is not giving up. He wants what he wants. The journey is long."

You don't say! I knew it before we went to war. Metaphysical warfare is consuming and hard on an individual.

I woke up a few hours later to introduce my head to the toilet bowl. I vomited the previous night's dinner and other things I cared not to see. Why torture myself when I didn't have to? While brushing my teeth, I saw my right eye was swollen shut. Goody. That business was back again. Nyanzira's witchcraft always left my eyes swollen. In those days, I saw it as confirmation of the metaphysical's existence and powers of manifestation into the physical. It meant this thing was real. I wasn't crazy.

Staring in the mirror at my swollen shut eye gave me the exact same feeling.

"It was a strong weapon," grandma mused.

True. I felt like I'd been dropped from a fifteen-storey building before a ten-ton truck ran over me. For good measure, it did it again. How many times had I gone through this with Nyanzira? Too many to count. What now?

"Gogo Ntombizodwa is going to teach you about herbs. You will be on the mat the whole day today."

How enchanting.

What I wanted was to spend the day on Netflix. I had readings the next day. I needed to conserve my energy for them.

"You will have the energy tomorrow. If you don't work on herbs today and create protective concoctions, you won't be there tomorrow to give your readings."

Got it. Would it be so bad not to exist?

"Yes. You have a purpose to fulfill. If you transcend without achieving it, God will bring you back to relive this life. You don't want that do you?"

Definitely not.

I lit the candles, made sure the tobacco plate was full and sat on the mat. Ripping one package open, I took a handful of the herb, clasped it tightly and closed my eyes.

"Gogo says this herb is very strong. It gets rid of evil and creates a protective barrier against anything dark. It also works on your clairvoyance. It makes what you see clearer."

Gogo was talking about Poke root.

"She says it requires absolute silence when in use. You program it only once and then let it do its thing. It's a seeker. It will go through your metaphysical and physical existence, pick out anomalies and work on them by itself."

I wrote it down on a label. I was going to put the herb in a jar afterwards.

"This is how you use it. You boil it. Steam yourself with it and then take a bath. You must also mop your whole house with the bathwater."

So much work!

"Let's move onto the next."

Mullen was a protective herb too. It worked in silence, like Poke. The difference in the two was Poke's aggressiveness, while Mullen was gentle. It took it's time and results were only 90 days after use.

"Put it aside. We need quick results at this moment. We're at war."

Agrimony was the thing. Hard-hitting as Poke, it had the power to return to sender. We desired its returning properties. The protective skills it possessed were nothing to be sneered at either.

Dragons blood was completely alien to my ancestors and it was a catalyst. It made spells stronger. We loved it.

Asafoetida, as unfamiliar as Dragon's blood gave gogo Ntombi as I took to calling her, orgasms. She was beside herself at its strength.

"It fights evil with everything! And then it protects. Nothing can get through this one. It is perfect in oils! You're going to make an oil out of it. You will use it every night until we say stop."

I wasn't enthused. Asafoetida stank.

"You will mix it with Lavender and other herbs. It won't smell bad."

Thank God for tiny little mercies.

By the time we were done, lots of hours later, we had herbs to bathe in, steam in, and use as lotion. I was to start right away.

Unfortunately for me, after herbal class where the herbs ended up talking directly to me, instead of via Gogo Ntombi, I couldn't get up. My energy was spent.

"Lay there. The mat will help heal you."

As I laid on the uncomfortable straw mat that my ancestors had used for centuries, for sex and childbearing, I closed my eyes and fell asleep, protected at my altar in the courts of the Bantu.

Chapter 12

3:00 am

Dancing with my ancestors.

My grandmothers were dancing with me. It was three in the morning and we were opening our court. My alarm goes off to a song by Oliver Mtukudzi called "Chiri Nani." This song, like most of his music is very spiritual. It speaks volumes to me. The lyrics are about the equality of every creature God made. There was nothing more superior than another, they said. It was therefore more important to ask for permission before taking or using it. The song also reminded people of ownership. Everything belonged to someone. Taking it without their permission was a crime against God.

I used to say to myself, "If only my family had asked me for my ancestors instead of trying to snatch them, my life would've been different. I wouldn't have suffered."

They didn't see me as an equal. They dehumanized me, something the song warned the people about, while attempting to strip me of everything. It was imperative for them to see me as subhuman. Oh, the memories as I danced.

My sister Linda, whom I adored and had a great relationship with, stunned me painfully one day when she looked me in the eye and said, "I have no problem killing you. It's a dog eat dog world. I won't feel remorse or guilt about it." Those were the last words she spoke to me. I haven't spoken to her in seventeen years. We will never ever talk again. We're strangers. With nothing in common. Not even blood.

The betrayal of a sibling you adore! At the time she declared me her enemy, I had no idea I was gifted. She was clued in when my mother indoctrinated her into the dark arts. I knew very little of what went on in my family. Shona people in general pride themselves on their ability to keep secrets. This might truly be a Bantu trait.

A whole village could plan for months to kill you and you wouldn't even know it. Chairman Mao initiated her little army right under my nose.

My sister's blatant rejection of me hurt deep. I didn't understand the hate. I was confused. It was tragic. The day before, we'd been talking and laughing with each other. I adored her. We shared a bedroom for years. I was her maid of honor at her wedding and accompanied her to her relentless secret missions to witchdoctors.

The change in her personality was drastic and permanent. I was devastated. She left me in tatters. What had I done to my little sister? It took me years to come to terms with the end of our relationship. Little did I know she stopped talking to me because she disowned me. I became food to her. She was after my metaphysical wealth because she had none of her own.

For years she succeeded at stripping me of my metaphysical wealth. She lived the high life, with twenty-four hour a day maid service, expensive schools for her daughters and a mansion one wouldn't believe. Yet, she didn't work hard enough, nor had any source of income which gave her the right to live this way.

She was brilliant at her job. So much so a witchdoctor once refused to see her. In fact, the witchdoctor stopped her while she was twenty-five kilometers away from her house. She sent an assistant to tell her to turn back.

"You're bringing too much evil," the assistant informed her and a companion.

At the time, Linda didn't believe she was evil. I mean, she wasn't doing anything other people were not doing. She insulated herself with reasons why she had to kill me. She was good. The witchdoctor who rejected her presence surprised her. She told everyone about it in amazement. I sympathized.

I've had to learn to listen to people when they talk. I mean really listen! People show you who they are from their words. To hear them, you must fight your preconceived opinion of the person.

They are a hindrance. My love for a sister I shared clothes with refused to let me see her for what she was. A killer.

I expect her to be even better at her job of wrecking people's lives with age. The coven my mother built doesn't tire. They're about their business twenty-four seven. If I slip up, they'll get me.

They're my inspiration. For real. Every time I think I'm too tired to push back against the dark, I remember how enthusiastic they are at what they do. I harness the same eagerness within me and get the job done.

An Indian witchdoctor, yes, we have African Indians and they're also in the continuum, once told me "People will betray you, especially the ones you love. Continuously, this will happen your entire life. Get used to it."

Funny how the pain is always the same. No one gets used to being eviscerated. "Chiri Nani" by Oliver reminded me that everything I was dying for was mine. As it was mine, no one else could have it.

I was the witchdoctor, the torchbearer, the shepherd of God's children. I was the seer, the harnesser of the elements, the one who lived between the veil and the physical world. I was the anointed. They couldn't take it away from me, no matter how much they tried. I felt empowered when I danced to Oliver Mtukudzi, an artist who died and came to me on the fourth day.

He didn't come for himself, because he went straight into the veil as a bright, blue energy. I watched him ascend. I was green with envy. He came for me, days later, because I was crying desolately and playing his songs in my damn bedroom.

"Chihera," he hailed me by my totem. "Why the tears?"

"It's too hard," I sobbed. I'd recently started using my gifts on YouTube in a bid to make them stronger. Talking to a culture which wasn't mine felt like climbing a mountain. Why was I doing it? Besides for selfish reasons that is. These people were never going to understand me. They were going to hurl abuse, make fun of me, break my heart. I felt vulnerable, broken.

If I could be like the other witchdoctors on YouTube who catered to their own, I would be happier. I would be safe. I wanted to stop. My ancestors wouldn't let me.

"This is easy," Oliver contradicted me. "I opened the door for you. You're spreading culture to those who were locked out due to no fault of their own. You know how it feels more than anyone. You've always been on the outside looking in. What you're doing is opening the door and inviting others into their own house."

"Why can't it be someone else?" Yes. That was the million-dollar question.

He laughed. "It is you! You're that someone. You're doing a great job. You're sitting in front of a camera and opening the courts for the world. This is something other witchdoctors would never do. Yes. There are other witchdoctors on YouTube. None of them give readings, nor do they share the intimacies of culture. They give a little. You give everything. Because you're the one who was picked to do so."

I breathed out. It was shaky business.

"Chihera?"

"Yes?"

"This is your destiny. There will be tears and pain. But the love you're going to receive is going to make up for everything. You will be embraced because you're sharing, healing, entertaining."

Yeah right.

"You will be better than me. When you pass your baton to the next generation, they will be in awe. They will say, "how did she do this?" Above all, those who listen to you and walk in your footsteps will be grateful."

As if!

"I did my part. You do yours." He went back to the veil.

Tears. They accompanied my dancing to "Chiri Nani" every time. The dancing released my pain, anger and hurt. The memories killed my soul. It wasn't easy to be born a sacrifice. I'd lost more than I gained. My sisters. I loved them dearly. They didn't give a hoot about me. They threw me away, like garbage.

They forgot the birthday parties I threw for them when it was taboo in our family to celebrate anything good. I would determinedly take money out of the family safe, invite their friends and cook all the food, including the birthday cake.

I introduced Christmas gifts and Christmas eve dinner. When I left, there was no more Christmas. Graduation parties were on me. I wrote the essays which got them into universities. What about the moments I walked them through job interviews? Not to mention the times I did their work for them when they were employed and couldn't make heads or tails of what was required.

They forgot me braiding their hair, cleaning up after them when they vomited or were too ill to move. Our household had very little compassion. They turned their backs on me after years of running to me for comfort and yes, love. No explanation was ever given.

"This is me!" I screamed in my head at them while doors slammed in my face, "the daughter our father said he resented because I was too family orientated!"

He said this, the day he told us how he felt about each one of his children. My sister Linda was his favorite because she was beautiful and ruthless. He adored Angie for her intellectual inability and her gift of not caring for family. Rumbi was a sensitive, selfish baby who never grew up. Milton was cruel and selfish. He deserved respect. I was the last he talked about.

"Isobel is the most family orientated. She would do anything for family. She has introduced Christmas and celebrating holidays to this household. She's constantly trying to get everyone to love each other. She sacrifices herself," he paused.

I fully expected him to say I was a great example to my siblings. Instead, he said, "I don't like her."

Everyone laughed hilariously.

"No, I don't like her," he repeated firmly. "There's no place for a child like her in my household."

More laughter.

I pretended I wasn't shocked or hurt. My dad was my absolute favorite parent. I adored him. He was my axis! And he threw me away. It eviscerated my soul. Basically, my dad was the first man to dump me.

Still, he was right. My sisters should've remembered what he said. Why didn't they fight for me the way I did for them? I never expected them to walk out of the room, leaving me completely alone. It hurt.

It took me a long time to realize it was okay to love people who didn't love you. I loved my sisters with a burning passion as I did my dad to the end. I wasn't going to stop. I loved Mark with everything. I was going to continue. I adored my friends. Whether they walked out of my life or not, I was going to hold onto to the love. Love never dies. It hurts more when you fight it. For that is unnatural. Loving is good. Don't ever stop. Love thy enemy. Just love yourself more.

When I dance with my ancestors, love trumps everything. Dancing with them is my favorite thing. It is a pure joy the physical world hasn't been able to replicate in my life. My greatest happiness, untainted, comes when I dance with them.

Gogo Ntombi is the best of the three of us. She has rhythm, although all she's doing is a Xhosa cultural dance to every song. She kicks her legs backwards with style and laughs hard. I try to copy her, give up, strike out on my own. I join in the laughter. My grandma isn't much of a dancer. She gives it her best shot. She mostly makes fun of me. She says I am like my gogo.

"You're a dancing fool like your gogo! At the drop of a hat, there you go!" she huffs. Yet, she dances with us anyway.

Gogo Ntombi is pure light filled with happiness. She was lucky to have led a human experience filled with love and respect. Married to the local chief, she had children who went on to travel the world and make babies with women from different cultures. There's no doubt my great grandparents were financially well off.

Moreover, Gogo Ntombi lived a life of great dignity as the local Igqirhakazi in the Eastern Cape of South Africa. When her time came, she passed through the veil in grace and honor, making it to the Peak. She was the only one of the three of us who knew happiness. She brought it into my life through dance.

That early morning, we put aside our war to stomp our feet, make faces, laugh hilariously at ourselves while we repeated Oliver Mtukudzi's song over and over. All my problems dissolved into my sweat and the air graciously evaporated them.

I began to feel strong, invincible. I was going to win this war because I had love on my side. I was therefore very energized and confident when I finally knelt on the mat, ready to launch missiles at our enemy.

"Musa!" I screamed, with my grandma's walking stick raised with both hands. "This household isn't ruled by men!"

Declaration of independence was important. I repeated it four times.

"This house, this life, in the metaphysical and the physical is run by me. A woman. I don't bow to a man, today, tomorrow, ever! Therefore, we've packed your weapons, evil spirits and your promises to yourself of owning me! We're sending them back to you! They're going to ravage you one hundred times more than you intended for me."

Once again, repeated four times. With every spell, one must make sure to include all the other baddies.

"I am returning all the weapons sent to me by Musa, and any others who are waging war against me double fold. I harness all the evil every single dark sided person put into the universe and am making them mine."

Repeated four times. My voice didn't waver, even at the extremely high octave required. The anger mounted, unbreakable. Good. I needed it.

"There will never come a time when someone will own, use or kill me because I am stronger than all of you. My ancestors, straight from the Peak where they resided next to God himself are older than all of yours."

I started to feel lightheaded. Semi possession came into play. Gogo Ntombi stepped into my energy. I lost myself in the big blue world. I loved it when I could float. It was a moment away from the hate. The feeling of freedom was short lived. I'd been sent into the veil by Gogo Ntombi to collect the weapons myself.

Energy bombarded me from all angles. I lost my mind in fear. I felt myself falling. The feeling was the same as if you are coming off a high diving board. Your stomach drops from under you, fear settles there, and then, relief when you hit the water.

In my case, there wasn't any water. There was my grandfather. His hand reached out for me from above. I grabbed it and held on as he lifted me up, removing me from the center of the energy. I laughed as I rose into the air. What joy!

The weapons followed behind me. I'd succeeded.

I came back to my time and to my grandma's voice. "Receive them with gratitude from the wind."

Another incantation. The weapons once again surrounded me. In the real world, they packed a malevolent and vicious punch. They blocked my air supply.

I can't breathe!

I felt I was going to pass out.

"Breathing isn't important."

You don't say!

"Talk to the weapons. Tell them, "weapons, sent to destroy others and have nowhere to go. You're now mine.""

I parroted grandma.

"Move to my walking stick,"" she continued the instruction. "Subjugate them."

I repeated it. Although I have no idea how I managed it in the fog.

"Lift the walking stick with both hands high above your head."

This order was a tall one for someone in my condition. I was barely teetering on my knees. Bombarded as I was with unknown forces, I couldn't move my limbs to do what I wanted them to.

"Lift the walking stick," grandma said it again.

With all the might I had left, I did it, head bowed.

"Head up, to the sky."

Posture corrected.

"Say, Musa, and everyone else who has hurt me, past, present and future, receive your gift."

I said it. The energy of all the dire creations of the dark witchdoctors circled my walking stick, releasing me from their grip. What a relief! The energy then shot up, taking some of me with it. I collapsed on the mat.

I woke up about fifteen minutes later to grandma's voice. "It is done and has been accepted. You did good."

How long was this going to take? I was worn out.

"Today you start bathing in herbs. You need to program them before we leave the court."

"What are we using?" There was no rest for the damned.

"Poke root."

I rose to retrieve it from the cupboard. I cupped as much as I could in my hand and knelt back on the mat. I was beginning to feel like I would never get off my knees. Grandma led me.

"Hail Mother Nature's child. Thank you for choosing us. We would like to ask you to use your purpose to cleanse us of evil.

Whether it came from the winds, the earth, water or fire, please wash it off us."

"Good job," grandma encouraged. "Your gogo says ask for protection."

"After you've made us clean, please protect us. Lock our doors in the metaphysical and in this world. Make sure no weapon created in my name reaches me. Keep the doors locked for eternity."

"Thank the herb."

"Thank you for choosing me. You're greater than I am, for you give of yourself more than I could."

Herbal baths began. Every day, it was a different herb. Some days, it was a concoction of herbs.

Was it working? God is good. He gave me proof. I dreamed of Musa when I went to bed. He was in a straight up wooden box with his head dangling out of it. His mouth was gagged and around him were metaphysical bars. The prison he intended for me was now his.

My onslaught had been successful. However, it would take several weeks for what had happened in the metaphysical to become three dimensional. In that time, he could pull a rabbit out of a hat. I wasn't out of the woods yet. Another dream confirmed that thought for me a few days later.

Chapter 13

The Dream.

"Girl, I had a dream about you," Agnes was all chirpy. It had nothing to do with the morning. Chirpy is her personality.

"Oh yeah?"

"Yeah. In the dream, you came to my house. You were looking tired yet elated. You said, Agnes, I've finished cleansing my house. My protective dome is up. Can you see it?"

"I could see it. Your house, the back and front yard, your entire property was encapsulated in a bright blue dome of light. It went all the way up to the sky.

"At last!" you said. "After suffering all these years, I've finally done it! Girl, I brought you some herbs to cleanse and protect your house too. Use them at once."

"You passed them onto me and left."

"OMG, confirmation my rituals are working." I was very pleased.

"I know," my bestie gushed. "These three people came knocking on my door. I let them in. They asked me what I was doing. I told them I was cleansing my house. At the time I was moping my floors with the herb you gave me.

They said, "why doesn't your friend help you? Aren't friends supposed to help each other?"

I was like, "She's tired. She just cleaned her whole house. Do you know Issey, we could see you sitting in your house, on the couch. The barrier of protection was still there though. They were not satisfied with my answer."

"Still," they said, "a friend should help another."

"What do you want?" I asked them.

"Well," they started laughing. "We were hoping you could take us to her place because we can't get in."

"No!" I said and they disappeared.

"Who were these people?" I wasn't concerned. I was still psyched about my barrier. "Do you have any idea?"

"They were not mine," Agnes was certain. "They were definitely Zimbabwean. Two men and a woman."

"How can you be sure they were Zimbabwean?"

"You Zimbabweans have your own mannerisms unique to you. We have ours. Definitely, they were your people. I think they tried to get into your house and failed. They came to me. They thought I would help them bust your barrier."

"What a weird dream. I'm going to put it to my ancestors."

I never did. The events which followed made me regret not doing so.

A few days later, I was just about to go to asleep. You know the moment when you're lying in bed, about to fall asleep, yet still hanging around? That's where I was, when I felt a tingly numbness all over my body. I couldn't move my legs. Then it was my torso, followed by the rest of me.

Shortly after, I felt myself being pulled up.

How was this possible? My body was glued to my bed. Yet, I was being lifted off it and out of my house.

I found myself in a home in Zimbabwe. The place resembled mine, although I could tell it wasn't. For one thing, it was too dark. Everything in the tiny fake living room was black and shadowy. There was a knock at the door. I went to answer it.

"May I come in?" Roseline asked.

I was speechless. The woman hadn't talked to me for years. In fact, she avoided me like the plague because of her habit of stealing my gifts and metaphysical assets for herself and her children.

"Let her in," grandma implored. "We need to talk to her."

I stepped aside. She sauntered in with a smile. The smile turned her into someone else who wasn't her. I was unbothered.

My cousin Wes stepped up. I was surprised. Roseline didn't know Wes. He was tete Retina's son, my dad's sister. There was no love lost between my maternal and paternal families. They didn't associate. So, what was Wes doing with Roseline? Odd. We stared at each other. I don't know who was more shocked. Him or me.

Suddenly, I was holding my grandfather's walking stick in my hand. Danger! My male ancestors only appear when I'm in peril.

This realization made me turn around to see what my aunt was doing. She was preparing something, a spell intended for me, no doubt. I was about to ask her what was up when my cousin gave a nervous laugh.

"I wasn't expecting to see you Gushungo."

"What?" I was puzzled. My grandfather was too.

The great Xhosa himself stepped up. "Did you call me Gushungo?"

My cousin got nervous. He stepped back. The other cousin, whose face I couldn't see, ran away.

"Am I Gushungo to you?" My ancestor was live and direct.

"Well, um," Wes stammered.

Meanwhile, my aunt was looking very deadly behind me. Whatever she had planned she was ready for it. She approached.

My grandfather interceded. "This ends now!"

The dream sequence came to a sudden halt. Except, it wasn't a dream. Re-entering one's body is a very painful experience. Your soul returns to its physical form starting with the legs. It slides in your body very slowly, and you feel the throbbing. It's like hot pins and needles making their way to your bone marrow. It takes time for your light to be fully ensconced inside you.

Moreover, your lower spine feels like you broke it a thousand times for several reasons. Your kidneys also want to escape their confinement and the nasty things choose your lower back as their exit point. It takes weeks for the agony to recede.

Thinking clearly takes a good few minutes too. The first few seconds of my brain power told me I'd had a nasty dream. The second decided I'd astrally projected.

"What?" I couldn't sit up. My lower back hurt like a mother-fucker.

"You were taken," grandma offered her knowledge. She was back. I was positive when I woke up, none of my ancestors were around. "into the veil."

"What?" I asked again, still confused.

"Since they couldn't get into your house, they took you out instead. The bangles. You were not wearing them."

"They gave me a rash."

"No. The ones who stole you gave you the rash. They knew you would take them off. It was preplanned, weeks in advance. We were consumed with Musa and didn't catch it."

Insecurity! Survivors of war, rape, violence of any kind know this feeling well. I wasn't safe anywhere. Oh my God, I hated my life. Why couldn't I have a normal existence like everyone else in the world?

"Gushungo," I whispered. "They saw Gushungo."

"We know."

What the fuck was he doing there? This was my life, forcefully astral projected or not. His presence endangered me for we weren't related. How did his ancestor become part of my soul? And why? The damn question I dreaded was back.

Gushungo's ancestor being recognized by another metaphysical scientist, albeit a dark one in a situation where it was supposed to be my ancestors and I alone had happened to me before, with dire consequences.

Nyanzira and Molly attached their ancestors to me in order to steal my gifts and yes, that dreaded metaphysical wealth. When being a part of me didn't bring them what they wanted fast enough,

213

their ancestors attacked mine. At the time, my ancestors were still getting on their feet. They lost the war. Both Nyanzira and Molly bagged them and threw them in their prisons. It left their ancestors running my life.

First consequence of having my ancestors stole was unexpectedly losing all my money and almost my house too. Furthermore, the world turned against me. It seemed like my city went crazy. My neighbors complained about my back yard. They said it was messy. Despite there being no evidence, I was charged thousands of dollars for not keeping my yard clean.

"I don't get it," the woman from the city said. "I inspected your yard six times and it was perfect. I think your neighbors are racist. They want you out of the neighborhood. I intended to ignore them, but they went to a member of parliament. Now I must charge you to make it look like I did something about it. I'm sorry."

I knew better. It wasn't racism. Something had gone wrong in my metaphysical world. Every dark person, regardless of race, who could come out to get me was doing it. The attacks seemed endless. Someone complained I was keeping my dogs outside. The police came and left after a gracious apology.

I received a letter from the garbage collectors, stating they would fine me if I didn't follow garbage collection rules. Again, an apology followed via the telephone a few days later.

It was accusation after accusation. Battle after battle. All wasting my money and time, as was the point. If I was busy fighting the world, I had no time for my metaphysical existence. The children of the ancestors who were running me could make my ancestors work for them without my objections.

When your world becomes too noisy, check your metaphysical first.

I found out Nyanzira stole my ancestors from my ancestors. About the same time the world was harassing me, Nyanzira did the final ritual to own them. He'd pushed enough random spirits my way to fill in the void they would leave, thereby hiding the theft from me and God.

It backfired. My ancestors, who were very clever people when they were alive, had a failsafe spell in place. If they were transferred to someone who wasn't blood, they immediately came to me in full force.

The reason it didn't happen when they were with my mother was because in our culture, a mother has full rights over their child and whomever or whatever is on the child. My mother was legally holding them. Go figure.

The first thing my ancestors told me was I needed help. Nyanzira had inundated me with a great deal of dark, powerful energy. Since I had absolutely no knowledge of how to get rid of it, it would take them time to bring me up to par. With the dark energy controlling me, it would be a difficult task. I was to find a witchdoctor to help me.

I got Molly through a friend. I flew to Zimbabwe to work with her. She helped me cleanse myself so my ancestors could fully function. Then she presided over my first ascension.

"You're safe now," she declared afterward. "The unrelated ancestors and dark spirits can no longer come to you because you've been ritualistically claimed by your own. Moreover, your ancestors are sitting more comfortably on their thrones."

She was right. The world came back on its axis again. Gone were my problems. I could breathe with ease.

Little did I know she'd attached her own ancestor, Shumba Mhazi to me during the ascension. Unlike Nyanzira's ancestors whom I never saw, I saw hers all the time. In my bedroom standing over me, at my random altars and when I took my dogs for a walk. He was everywhere! I believed he was protecting my ancestors and I, so I didn't worry. I even saw him as a source of comfort. He was my friend's ancestor after all.

My world turned topsy turvey again. I fell ill. Molly demanded thousands of dollars to help me. When I couldn't come up with it fast enough, I got worse. If it wasn't for the good nosey spirit, I would've died.

I got rid of Shumba Mhazi by myself. I chanted for absolute weeks, until he gave up and walked away.

This Gushungo thing was therefore as bad as astral projection. He couldn't be hunting me along with the others, could he? I denied it. I didn't want to scream in agony.

Not him, my mind insisted. He was a witchdoctor of Light. I enjoyed talking to him. He taught me many useful rituals. His rites were all earth bound. He used soil, stones, rice, corn meal. The hardest thing he ever told me to do was to feed the birds. He couldn't have a hand in darkness. He couldn't.

There were numerous other usual suspects. It could've been my mother and her sisters. After all, Roseline was the one who walked into the house in the veil. Or, my brother Milton and his sisters. Taurai and his mother Juliet couldn't be counted out either. Or my aunt Retina and her sons, Wes and Les. They could've used Gushungo's essence.

Wait a minute. It didn't make sense. The three people were as surprised by Gushungo's presence as my ancestors and I were. He wasn't expected, by any of us. Wes was the one who recognized Gushungo in the astral projection tableau. In real life, he knew Gushungo. He would recognize the spirit on me because he'd met the man. If that were true, it meant the man who stood at the door after they astrally projected me was my cousin Wes. He wasn't a cover for the real culprit.

How could this be? I was confused.

"We will get to the truth," grandma announced. "Rest."

Not on this bed, I decided. For the umpteenth time in my life, I vacated my bedroom for the couch.

My grandmas and I spent the next day going through the entire experience, bit by bit. The devil is in the details. We looked for mistakes in the metaphysical scene the threesome who stole me put together.

The meeting with the three happened in the veil. We agreed grandfather pulled me out of the veil. But, not before Gushungo usurped his place for a few seconds.

"We shall ask Gushungo what he was doing there when the time comes," grandma said. "At all times, when a war is begun because of one enemy, all the others rise as well. We expected it."

"Gushungo," I whispered in tears. My heart was breaking. Oh my God, this stupid heart! All it did was break. Please, don't let him be my enemy. I couldn't fight him. He touched my soul.

"He will tell us why he was with us and then we will know if he is your enemy. We're not worried about him. We know who he is."

"Who are you worried about?" If they weren't bothered with Gushungo, it might mean he had good reasons to escort me. It lightened my heart.

"The three people who astral projected you."

Although I recognized two faces, Roseline and Wes, I knew the dark side wore people's faces to mask their true identities.

"You said in the veil I was to let her in. You wanted to talk to her."

"Yes. The essence of the woman was my daughter, Retina."

Oh God up above. Not my aunt! She was the last link to my family. When everyone else walked out of the room, she stayed. I once cried to her that no one loved me. She replied, "I love you. Your life means everything to me."

I believed her. So, I clung to her. In her home, I was at peace.

I also contribute to her care. A diabetic, she needs very expensive medicine. I go without so she can have what she needs to survive.

"It means nothing," grandma's gentle voice wafted to my ears. "Essences are stolen all the time. For the moment however, we have to go with what we saw."

"She came with her sons?" I asked dully.

It made sense. Wes was the one who recognized Gushungo. No one else knew Gushungo, except him because I met Gushungo with Wes.

This sucked on a huge scale. I liked Wes. I helped give him a career. I literally semi prostituted myself for him to be accepted as an apprentice at the company where I worked. The career saw him traveling around the world. It also gave him a lot of money. I was invested in his life.

As for his older brother, we never liked each other. His betrayal didn't hurt.

"Yes. We will call her, hear what she has to say. First things first. Get our plate, fill it with water and bring it to the altar."

I retrieved my grandma's wooden plate from the cupboard, filled it with water and came back to the mat.

"Put some tobacco in the water. Hail Gushungo. Ask him to reveal himself as you wash your hands in the water."

I did so.

"Now, go and pour the water outside, on the ground, very slowly, facing the west."

I scrambled up and ran outdoors.

The atmosphere changed in my unfinished basement a few minutes after I sat back on the mat. The energy was non-threatening and very controlled.

"Walking stick!" grandma urged.

I grabbed and held it in both hands. I knew the drill. I never faced an energy unrelated to me. I was to always give them my back and say nothing. Conversations between ancestors remained between them for security reasons.

Seeing my face or hearing my voice could enable the unrelated ancestor to steal my essence. Without your essence, you're pretty much fucked.

"Gushungo," my grandma began in respectful, restrained tones. I knew she was angry. She impressively held it in check. "You have arrived."

"Indeed." There was no emotion, one way or another. It was difficult to say whether he was a friend or an adversary.

"What were you doing with our child in the veil?"

"Protecting her. The males with her are still weak. They take a long time to react, due to the machinations of her people. Had I not been there, they wouldn't have stepped up. As it was, I'm the one who alerted them to the danger of their child having been pulled into the veil. My help was requested a few weeks ago. I provided."

I remembered asking Gushungo for help when the Story Teller was stolen. He said he would go up the mountain to talk to his ancestors for they were people who loved higher ground. I hadn't spoken to him since.

My grandmas and I also knew we did a ritual right after the Story Teller came back to let Gushungo know we no longer needed his help. We were closing ourselves off from outside interference. Had Gushungo not heard us?

Perhaps he had already sent one of his ancestors to us in good faith.

"We would like to thank you in gratitude," my grandma was cold. Her reaction made me all the way nervous. "At this point, we are asking you to step back. Your assistance is no longer required."

"No."

222

Boom! And a new experience for me. An unrelated ancestor was refusing to leave!

"Why not?"

"I will leave when my job is done."

"It is done." Grandma was firm.

"Not yet. This is a long war. One your child could lose. You need my help."

"We don't want it."

"That's unfortunate." He disappeared.

"Now what?" I asked my grandma.

"Allow gogo Ntombi, your grandfathers and I to consult for a moment."

I believed Gushungo's ancestor. He was there to help me. My grandfathers were difficult ancestors. They worked in the shadows. The Story Teller was always being stolen and I resented him for it. Why couldn't he hang, like my grandmothers? I barely knew the other one. We always met in the veil and words were never exchanged. In the veil, I loved him intensely because I felt his unreserved love towards me. In the veil, we connected at a level I didn't share with my grandmothers or the Story Teller.

In the physical, however, he was distant. He possessed my body when he needed to do something in the physical world and then just as quickly, disappeared. I felt him around me though, sometimes, from a distance.

I knew he was the boss. Everything went through him. It was him who decided my grandma would be the main spokesperson. It was also him who made all the major decisions in my life, including choosing my lovers.

As powerful as he is, he was also the most fragile. Like me, he was on everyone's hit list. There wasn't a living relative or stranger who came across me who didn't want to snatch him. My mother succeeded spectacularly. If it wasn't for the betrayal of her compatriot Nyanzira and Taurai, she would still have held him.

As it was, Nyanzira promised him to Taurai at an exorbitant fee. For two years Taurai believed he had the great Xhosa. He wore my grandfather's ancestral colours and woke up early every morning to chant to him, completely setting aside his own ancestors. Taurai was extremely consistent. He attributed every little success in his life to my ancestor and got rabidly obsessive to the point of asking Nyanzira to kill me.

Poor Taurai. He never had my ancestor. He imagined he did. He therefore lived the life.

What really happened was, Nyanzira wrestled the great Xhosa from my mother. He did the ritual for him to arrive to me. And then he began the battle to take him away for himself. He succeeded in destroying our link. He didn't in harnessing my grandfather.

A human sacrifice, other than me, was required for Nyanzira to get my grandfather. Nyanzira had the best candidate. Taurai. He was in the process of setting it into motion while still trying to trap my grandfather's energy when he triggered the failsafe. My grandfather came back to me.

Unfortunately, the numerous blockages and theft took their toll. The process of mending them took time. We were mired in rituals of resurrection and merging without end. Our last rituals took place in Zimbabwe with the help of five witchdoctors, Gushungo and Musa included.

We were therefore getting to know each other in the middle of this war. I had no idea what his personality was like. I also had to still experience the gifts he brought which made everyone fight for him. He apparently has venerable gifts, rare and unique.

I know his story in little bits and pieces. He was my great grandfather even though I referred to him as grandfather. There's no word in my language for great grandfather. He was the son of a Xhosa chief, husband to Ntombizodwa, dad to my grandfather. I saw his face twice, once in a dream and another time when his energy wafted around me. Both occasions were brief.

A water baby, he loved the ocean and spent his days as a young man staring at it from a cliff in the Eastern Cape. He died away from home. That's all I had.

In my bitter moments, I could believe he needed to be prodded to protect me as Gushungo said. There were times I thought he wasn't good at protecting me. My grandma insisted otherwise. She was backed by numerous witchdoctors. Without him I would be dead, they said. His defence and protection of me was like no other. I had too many enemies, more than the usual Chosen had to deal with. Even so, in my worst times, it was hard to believe.

My understanding times, however, brought sympathy and insurmountable love for him. Of all my ancestors, he had it the worst as he was the most desired.

The dark side made his journey very difficult. They fought him viciously, sometimes with great success. My mother and Nyanzira brought him to the very dark door of the veil. He battled his way back to me. His sorrow, which I sometimes feel, is deep. He says people have become so cruel. My grandma says they always were.

My grandfather was the strongest of us all. Our love for each other, never in doubt, even in my days of resentment, was our rock. He would never let anything happen to me. He was my blood.

No. This Gushungo wasn't there to protect me. I was no longer in doubt.

"Your grandfather says he pushed Gushungo out of your soul in the veil. He had not seen him until then. Gushungo camouflaged himself very well. We unveiled him in the net."

When doing spells and rituals directed at an individual, we always make a wider net. We include anyone else who may be up to the same business as our enemy. This produces interesting results. Sometimes, we learn the person we were defending ourselves against was small fry to another we had no idea about.

"Something we did broke his cover. He was as surprised at being called by the one at the door as we were." Grandma came back with news.

I started to cry. I felt awful for my grandfather and I. He could only be as resilient as I was. He needed to be reinforced by me. At least, we were together now. We had time to fortify and get to know each other.

"He is not a friend," grandma continued of Gushungo. "We have found another enemy. And this enemy is inside our home."

My world crumbled to bits.

"He is here, because he wants something of yours. The same thing Musa wants. The technique and style he used is different. That's why he managed to get this far. We're going to have to get rid of him."

Fuck it, fuck it, fuck it!! Why?

"You're a dragon. The mistress of earth, wind, fire and water. You're the one percent. Musa is water. Gushungo is earth and wind. They want to rise in the ranks. By taking from you."

Okay. Breathe in, breathe out. Let it sink in, no matter how much it hurts. Coming to terms with truth is the first step in winning the battle.

"Never talk to Gushungo again."

Undoubtedly.

"As for the three people. They came to us as Retina and her sons. It makes sense, when you take into context the fact that you lived with them when you went to Zimbabwe. It therefore made it possible for them to make you allergic to your bangles in order to astral project you."

Oh no. The only family I had left.

"Nevertheless, we don't know if it is them. This was a very good cover. They deserve the benefit of the doubt. They have to physically own up to their crime."

"How are they going to do it?" I felt compassion for my grandmother. Tete Retina was her baby. She cherished her. This was as hard for her as it was for me.

"Gogo says call your aunt and cousins. Tell them you had a dream. Describe it exactly the way it happened. Leave out the astral projecting and what we know. Her soul, on this earth will tell us whether it was her and her sons or not."

"What about Agnes' dream? How does it fit in?"

"The same three people could've visited Agnes first, before coming to you. Or, it could be a different set of people. We're going to go with a different set of people."

"Grandma?" I paused.

"Yes?"

"Does this mean our war is being fought on four fronts?"

"Yes."

To be continued......

Made in the USA
Monee, IL
06 February 2020

21392199R00128